A Teachers' Guide
to the
Psychology of Learning

for Sylvia

A Teachers' Guide
to the
Psychology of Learning

Michael J. A. Howe

Basil Blackwell

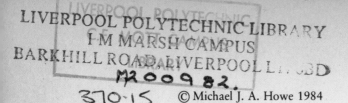
© Michael J. A. Howe 1984

First published 1984

Basil Blackwell Publisher Limited
108 Cowley Road, Oxford OX4 1JF, England

Basil Blackwell Inc.
432 Park Avenue South, Suite 1505
New York, NY 10016, USA

British Library Cataloguing in Publication Data

Howe, Michael J. A.
    A teachers' guide to the psychlogy of
    learning.
    1. Learning, Psychology of   2. Educational
    psychology
    I. Title
    370.15'23   LB1060

ISBN 0-631-13577-4
ISBN 0-631-13578-2 Pbk

Typeset by Oxford Publishing Services
Printed in Great Britain by
Camelot Press Ltd, Southampton

Contents

Preface

All teachers should be experts in human learning. As well as having practical expertise, teachers need to know about those scientific advances in knowledge of the mechanisms and causes of learning that can be applied to the vital job of helping children and adolescents to learn.

This book is about the contributions of modern cognitive psychology to our understanding of those kinds of learning that are necessary for making progress in the school classroom. The book concerns itself with the acquisition of the cognitive abilities that enable a young student to become educated. The emphasis is on the learning of intellectual skills and forms of knowledge that are based on language: there is stress on the kinds of basic skills that make literacy and numeracy possible.

Applying the findings of psychological research into cognition leads to very real increases in learning. Teachers can help their students to become more efficient and more effective as learners. This is made possible by a knowledge of how the varied causes of learning exert their influence and contribute to success at school.

Because psychological approaches to educational matters are so varied it may be useful to specify what this book is *not* designed to achieve. It is not a general textbook on educational psychology; the content is restricted to learning, remembering and related processes. The book has not much to say about particular instructional curricula or about the teaching of specific school subjects: it is not about 'how to teach'. Nor does the book attempt to survey comprehensively the large and growing body of psychological and educational research into learning: it is not a handbook of psychological or educational research. Finally, the book does not give any emphasis to the 'theories of learning' that experimental psychologists invented in the first half of this century. This might seem a surprising exclusion. The main reason is that such theories have very little application to any remotely practical questions about the acquisition of the kinds of abilities that children learn at school.

I have deliberately been selective. Decisions about choice of content have reflected the needs of the classroom teacher. Some of the contents will benefit the teacher by providing increased knowledge of learning that can be directly applied to everyday classroom learning. Other contents may be less directly applicable but will give the reader a fuller understanding to draw upon.

I would like to thank all the colleagues and friends at the University of Exeter who in one way or another have helped to make it possible for me to write this book.

Introduction

It is easy to say that learning is important, but its very familiarity can lead us to forget how total is our dependence on being able to learn. In and out of school, learning is a major force in almost every aspect of human life.

Stop reading for a moment and make a mental list of any four things you have done today. Any activity will do. Did any of them *not* depend upon learning? It is highly unlikely, since learning contributes to virtually everything a person does. Even the most basic human activities, eating and drinking, for example, have learned elements. A newborn infant can neither chew nor hold a knife and fork!

Everyone learns, and up to a point everyone knows how to learn. Any educated person has some degree of insight into the causes of human learning. Teachers require more than this, however. They are expected to be experts in learning, specialists who can use their knowledge and skills in order to help others to learn. Teachers benefit from any progress that is made towards gaining increased understanding of human learning processes, so long as that progress can be translated into genuinely practical knowledge about how children acquire the kinds of abilities they need to learn at school.

What are the Causes of Human Learning?

Teachers and others are always looking for ways to improve learning. We want to find ways to learn more efficiently and more effectively. The solutions must partly lie in knowing about the *causes* of human learning. The more that is known about the factors that help a person to learn, the better placed we shall be to bring about practical increases in people's learned achievements.

That sounds simple enough. In fact, of course, there are many complications. One source of difficulty is that numerous factors can influence learning. Consider the following conversation about nine-year-old Charlie, who is not having much success at school. In the teachers' room the staff are trying to explain Charlie's lack of progress.

'It's because he can't concentrate,' suggests his class teacher.

'I think it is more a matter of his lack of interest,' replies a colleague.

'It's not that: he just does not try. He's bone idle,' says someone else.

'His family background is all wrong; his older brother never did well at school.'

'That can't be the explanation: Charlie's sister was top of her class.'

'There you have it: girls learn more than boys at that age.'

'I think he lacks basic ability. He's doing the best he can but he is a slow learner.'

'But he is a terrific soccer player. Doesn't that require a real ability to learn?'

'But that is different. Soccer is a motor skill, and completely different from school learning.'

'The trouble with Charlie is that he missed a term, two years ago, and he's never really caught up.'

'No, that's not the basic problem. He fell on his head when he was a baby, and he must have suffered brain damage which reduced his capacity to learn.'

'But it is not just Charlie who is failing. None of the children we teach these days are keen to learn.'

'That is because teachers become less enthusiastic and less effective as they get older.'

'Speak for yourself! I blame television: it fills their brains with rubbish and makes school learning impossible.'

'I think you are all wrong. The real problem is that the parents don't care.'

'That may be true, but they don't feel at home in the school environment, and they don't know how to prepare their children for school.'

At this point Charlie's teacher had to leave, but the discussion continued as soon as her back was turned.

'It's her own fault. Her classes are so boring that Charlie is just not motivated.'

'That's partly right: she does not allow for individual differences. She treats the children as if they were all the same, and that doesn't suit Charlie.'

'I think Charlie is slightly deaf, and with all that noise going on he can't hear what his teacher says.'

'It's not that. The teacher is too strict: her kids do not discover things for themselves.'

'Nonsense! She's not strict enough. There is no control in that classroom and no structure. Consequently the children learn nothing. They don't know what they are supposed to be doing.'

Each one of the above remarks provides some kind of attempt to state the cause of Charlie's failure to learn. They are a cross-section of the kinds of explanations that people commonly offer. We might regard them as being very crude *theories* of learning (or, strictly speaking, failing to learn). At its simplest, a theory consists of the ideas – good or not so good – that have been put forward in order to explain something. Some of the suggestions may have struck you as being quite sensible, and others less so. You would probably agree that even among those views that you thought most pertinent no one of them provided a complete explanation. Learning is influenced by a large number of different factors.

Whatever we may think of the quality of the views expressed in the teachers' conversation, it is clear that there was no shortage of ideas about the causes of learning and of failure to learn. Even if only half of the items suggested by Charlie's teachers do actually influence learning, it is clear that obtaining a full account of learning and its causes cannot be a simple task.

To complicate matters even further, the different influences interact with one another: they do not act in isolation. In order to gain an understanding of school learning which includes a satisfactory account of its causes, it is essential to find a way to reduce the complexities. Otherwise, if we are not careful, our efforts to explain learning and make practical improvements will be overwhelmed by the sheer quantity of the contributing influences.

Effects of Students' Activities and Prior Knowledge

Fortunately, we can clarify matters considerably by imposing a very simple classification of the main influences upon school learning. By concentrating upon those factors that have a *direct* effect on learning, it is possible to reduce the many different influences to two broad categories of events. The first category consists of activities that the learner undertakes. That is to say, what a person learns is largely determined by what that individual *does*. The second category of influences upon school learning is the learner's existing knowledge: what a person learns is also strongly influenced by what that individual already *knows*.

Some of the activities that result in learning will be described in chapters 2 and 3. They can take various forms: examples are rehearsal, categorizing and the use of effective retrieval skills. Always, however, some kind of mental processing takes place. Information that is perceived by the learner is subjected to cognitive activity that results in a modification to the individual's capacities: something new has been learned.

The processing activities that lead to learning may be performed deliberately, but on other occasions they can be entirely automatic. Similarly, the learner may be conscious of invoking a cognitive plan or strategy, and have a definite intention to so, or he may be totally unaware that any cognitive processing is taking place. On some occasions the mental processes that result in learning may be elements in a complicated plan or a highly organized strategy that is being undertaken by an educated learner who is very conscious of wanting to learn something and well equipped with learning skills and knowledge of effective procedures. In other instances the same mental processes may be activated by a person's attempts simply to make sense of newly perceived information, without any plan, strategy or intention to learn being involved.

The learner's existing knowledge forms the second of the two major direct influences upon school learning. (The word 'knowledge' is used here in the broadest sense, to include anything that a person 'knows', factual or otherwise, correct or incorrect, and beliefs and attitudes as well as straightforward information.) Learning is powerfully affected by what the learner already knows. An individual's existing knowledge, acquired through past experience, makes it possible for that person to understand new information and new events.

Two children's perceptions of the 'same' events may be quite dissimilar, because differences in prior knowledge, determined by past learning experiences, lead to contrasting interpretations being placed on objectively identical perceptual inputs. Chapter 4 describes some of the research that has investigated the effects of a person's existing knowledge on new learning, and looks at the implications of this research for learning in the classroom.

Emphasizing the importance for school learning of students' own activities ('What the learner does') and existing knowledge ('What the learner already knows') directs our attention to the attributes of the *individual* human learner. Unless we pay such attention, very little progress can be made towards understanding or improving school learning. An understanding of the central place of individuals' cognitive activities helps us to deal with various problems and issues in education. For example, in the fairly recent debate concerning the relative merits of *discovery learning* (whereby the teacher attempts to provide learning environments in which the student can 'discover' new knowledge) and *reception learning* (in which the teacher presents the information to the student, who simply 'receives' it), it is helpful to remember that learning depends entirely upon the mental activities of the learner. Whatever the teacher does is only important insofar as it affects the student's mental actions.

Although we have distinguished between a person's existing knowledge and the same individual's mental activities and strategies, in practice the two factors are closely related and interdependent, and often inseparable. This is particularly apparent in the context of the cognitive skills necessary for learning, thinking and remembering. For instance, a child's ability to make use of the fact that two plus two equals four might equally well be seen as an arithmetical *activity* or as evidence that the child *knows* something. However, so long as we bear in mind the fact that such ambiguities do exist it is extremely useful, for practical purposes, to classify the main direct influences on learning into instances of either the learner's activities or the learner's previous knowledge.

Indirect Influences on School Learning

You have probably noticed that in describing learners' activities and learners' prior knowledge as being *the* causes of learning we appear to have excluded all the other possible influences, including many of those to which Charlie's teachers drew attention. However simple and elegant the system of classification, it can hardly be entirely satisfactory if it excludes most of the major influences! What about the effects of attention, boredom, interest and so on? What of the psychological concept of motivation, and the effects of rewards and incentives? And what about the other influences mentioned by the teachers, including perceptual disorders such as deafness, family background and social class, and the possible effects of hereditary factors?

Of course these are all important, and they are not ignored in this book. But their influence on learning differs from that of learners' activities and learners' knowledge in one crucial respect. Essentially, these additional factors affect learning *indirectly*, whereas activities and knowledge have a *direct* influence. Motivational factors, for example, can exert their effects upon learning by encouraging the individual to undertake appropriate processing activities and strategies. The effects of attending can be similar: close attention to the task raises the probability of the learner carrying out appropriate activities and making use of existing knowledge that is relevant to the task. Reinforcing events, likewise, can influence a person's behaviour, and thus, indirectly, help determine what is learned.

Another major influence on learning is *teaching*. But, again, the effects are relatively indirect. Good teaching will increase the likelihood of a student acting in such a way that learning takes place. The teacher can also direct the student's attention to those aspects of existing knowledge that will help to make new information understandable. Yet it is always the learner who does the learning, not the teacher! However skilled the teaching, if it does not lead to the student undertaking appropriate processing activities, no learning can take place.

The undoubtedly important effects upon learning of factors such as *family background* and *social class* are also indirect. Circumstances of family life help determine the kinds of environmental events to which a child is exposed. But even so, the direct causes of the child's learning lie in the manner in which the individual child actually processes the information about these events that is perceived by the child. So far as learning and remembering are concerned, much depends upon the *meaning* of the events for the particular child who perceives them. This, in turn, largely depends upon the individual's existing knowledge.

People sometimes speak rather glibly of *the environment* as a major influence on learning. Of course environmental influences are crucial, but it is essential to recognize that when we use the term 'the environment' what we actually mean is the environmental events that are perceived by a particular individual, and as interpreted by that particular person. Placing two children in the same place at the same time does not guarantee equivalent environmental influences. They may attend to and perceive different aspects of the situation. Even when they both attend to the same things they may perceive and interpret them quite differently, in ways that largely depend upon the existing knowledge and mental skills of each individual child. So far as human learning is concerned, there is really no such thing as *the* environment: a child's environment is partly a product of the unique knowledge and mental processing of that individual child.

The various possible influences on learning of *hereditary factors*, although incompletely understood, are also probably indirect. It has been suggested that there might exist hereditarily determined differences in 'learning rate', related to physiologically measurable differences in rates of processing by the human brain, but scientists have not produced any firm evidence for assertions of this kind (Thompson, 1976). It is more likely that genetic factors can have a number of indirect effects on learning, via individual differences between people in such factors as perceptual sensitivity, attending behaviours, temperament or traits such as 'impulsivity' (Korner, 1971; Escalona, 1973). Some of these factors are known to be genetically transmitted.

The statement that learning is an active process is quite literally true. We sometimes forget this, perhaps because the activities that produce learning are often automatic and take place without the individual's awareness. In fact, it is quite wrong to believe that learning can ever be a simple process of passive absorption. School learning cannot take place in the absence of considerable mental-processing activity, conscious and deliberate or otherwise, on the part of the person who learns. Learning *always* involves (mental) doing.

Learning Takes Many Forms

The single word 'learning' seems to refer to one phenomenon, or one kind of process. In fact that is not the case. Like many other single words, 'health', 'weather' or 'prosperity' for example, the term 'learning' is actually applied to a wide range of different phenomena, many of which have little in common with the others.

For instance, in the course of a year a child may learn to tie her shoelaces, to enjoy eating cabbage, the names of the days of the week, to smile at Uncle Max, not to take sweets from strangers, that her birthday is in a month named January, to turn on the tap, that 'duck' is the name of a flying animal in a story-book, the numbers up to ten, that two plus one makes three, that lighted candles go out if you blow them, the names of various children, adults and pets, not to play with matches, that crying is often a successful ploy, the best way to increase the probability of Grannie providing some chocolate, and many, many other things besides.

The essential point is that the occasions, circumstances, forms and contents of learning are not simply numerous but also extremely varied. The term is applied very widely, to phenomena that differ from one another in many ways. In trying to explain learning, therefore, the task is to understand not one thing but a very broad category of things, containing a large range of differing kinds of events.

In the classroom, it is often desirable that the teacher should be able to specify clearly and precisely what it is that students are expected to learn. That is, the teacher should be clear about the *objectives* of instruction. Practical assistance with clarifying learning objectives is provided by the *Taxonomy of Educational Objectives* that was devised by Benjamin Bloom and others (Bloom, 1956). The taxonomy categorizes objectives into six classes: *knowledge, comprehension, application, analysis, synthesis* and *evaluation*. It also provides examples and illustrative material that can help a teacher to verify whether or not the outcomes of student learning match the teacher's intentions.

It can also be useful to categorize the *different forms of learning* that take place. For example, Robert Gagne (1970) distinguishes between eight types of human learning, ranging from simple associations between items to the relatively complex forms of learning necessary for concept formation and problem solving. Since the actual forms that learning takes are numerous and varied, any simple classification system inevitably introduces a degree of arbitrariness, but the classifying excercise serves as a valuable reminder that not all forms of learning are identical, or even similar to one another.

Do all the varieties of learning have anything in common? It is certainly true to say that all forms of learning share one important attribute: they all involve some kind of alteration or change in the learner. All attempts to provide definitions of learning refer to this. But when scientists attempt to define learning more precisely, and try to be more explicit about the particular kinds of changes that do or do not constitute learning, they quickly run into difficulties. Do the changes have to be ones that affect the individual's behaviour? Perhaps so, but only if we include thoughts, beliefs, wishes and attitudes as instances of behaviour. In that case the phrase 'a change in behaviour' becomes too broad and inexplicit to add any real precision to the meaning of learning.

Even at the level of the underlying physical mechanisms, it has not proved possible to identify any single set of physiological processes that are common to all instances of human learning. Many neuroscientists have tried to identify such a set of physical processes and changes in the brain – known as the *engram* of learning – but they have had little success (Thompson, 1976). One of the reasons is that at the physiological as well as the psychological level of explanation the various phenomena which share the term 'learning' are actually very different from one another in many ways.

Are all forms of learning useful and necessary? Does learning always help the individual to survive or to adapt to the circumstances of life? Many instances of learning are certainly valuable for the individual; they do help a person adapt to life's demands. In many species and in primitive man many learned abilities can be seen to help the individual to survive, although for people in developed societies a person's chances of staying alive are not usually quite so dependent upon everyday learning. However, some of the things that people learn do not seem to meet any real need or provide a useful function. For example, I have learned that the third house on the nearby road is called 'Bel-Vista', a piece of information which is unlikely to have the slightest value for me, at any time in my life!

The above instance could equally well be regarded as one of remembering as one of learning. Psychologists have often tried to make a distinction between learning and remembering, along the lines that learning primarily involves acquisition, whereas remembering is largely a matter of retention. In fact, however, tasks of learning and tasks of remembering each depend upon a number of mutually overlapping processes, and in many school instruction contexts the two terms are interchangeable. Ask yourself, for example, is it more accurate to speak of a child *learning* a poem or an unfamiliar grammatical rule, or *memorizing* it? It really makes no difference.

Of course, in everyday life it is often useful to distinguish between learning and memory. However, from the point of view of psychologists who are interested in understanding learning and knowing about the influences that cause it, the distinction is somewhat illusory. The causes of school learning and the processes and mechanisms that underlie it are by no means separate or distinct from the causes of remembering.

Many of the early theories of learning that were put forward by psychologists were based on research involving non-human species, notably rats, and were largely concerned with the simple kinds of learning, or *conditioning*, whereby behaviour is altered, as in *operant conditioning*, or associations are formed between perceived events, as in *classical conditioning*. These forms of associative learning were regarded by some early theorists in the behaviourist tradition as forming the 'building blocks' for the more complex forms of learning that take place at school. It is now accepted that although simple forms of conditioning do have a role in human life their relationship to school learning is somewhat distant (Howe, 1980). In order to understand how children acquire the abilities they gain at school it is necessary for researchers to investigate those kinds of learning that are involved in the cognitive tasks a child actually encounters at school. It is not enough to make statements about school learning that are really based on research into much simpler forms of learning.

School Learning

There is no clear line of demarcation between 'school learning' and other varieties of learning, but it is broadly true that at school certain forms of learning receive more attention than others. School learning usually involves the use of language. The school curriculum gives prominence to the acquisition of general-purpose symbolic skills such as reading and arithmetic, and to knowledge and abilities that depend on these skills. Of course, much school learning depends upon the child having abilities that were gained before starting school, such as basic language competence. Conversely, much of the knowledge that is acquired at school, and most of the skills, are intended to contribute to the learning of further knowledge and further abilities, in and out of school.

Cumulative and hierarchical aspects

Most of what a child learns at school is cumulative. It builds on previous learning and contributes to future learning. We noted earlier that a person's existing knowledge, gained through previous experience, is a powerful influence upon new learning. (Chapter 4 will examine in greater detail the effects of what the learner already knows.) Quite often, gaining an important ability may require the learner to master a number of sub-skills, organized hierarchically at a number of separate levels, with mastery of the higher levels depending upon the learner having previously gained essential lower-level abilities.

For practical purposes, it can be very useful to represent the steps that a learner needs to master in order to acquire a learned ability as forming a hierarchy of skills (Gagne, 1970). At the bottom of the hierarchy are abilities that the student already possesses. At the top is the eventual skill to be acquired, and on the intervening levels are the successively more difficult steps via which the eventual learning goal can be achieved.

The hierarchical organization of the different abilities is especially important in learning mathematics and learning to read. In mathematics instruction it is particularly important for curriculum design to take careful account of the sequencing of instructional materials. It is obviously important to specify the initial state of the learner's skill and knowledge, and to begin instruction from this base (Glaser, 1982). From that point, the abilities to be acquired can be described as forming a hierarchy in which the bottom level depicts initial abilities, and the top point describes the eventual object of instruction, and the intervening levels represent successively more advanced skills, each of which depends upon those abilities described in the lower levels. Depicting existing abilities, target skills and intervening skills in this way makes it possible to design appropriate sequences of instruction. Designing classroom instruction on this basis has proved to be a highly effective procedure for mathematical and scientific education (Gagne and Dick, 1983; White, 1979).

Reading is another learned achievement which requires the individual to acquire and build upon a number of different sub-skills, and to bring various kinds of knowledge and a number of skills together in the appropriate manner. It is hardly surprising that some children have great difficulty learning to read: the number of things that a person has to learn in order to be able to read, and the added difficulties of having to bring together the different kinds of contributing knowledge and the different sub-skills, make the total learning task a large and difficult one. That the majority of children do learn to read at a fairly young age suggests that many teachers of young children possess remarkable instructional abilities. Reading is rarely acquired spontaneously, and among the instances of learning that it depends on are ones for which people are ill equipped, such as combining *duh*, *o*, and *guh* to form the word *dog*. In instances such as this, learning is made difficult by the fact that doing so actually produces *duh-o-guh*, however fast the three parts are blended (Rozin, 1976).

Mastery learning

Because learning is cumulative, with future success at learning tasks being heavily dependent on existing knowledge and skills, acquired through previous experience, a student's incomplete mastery of school learning tasks can have damaging consequences for learning in the future. For this reason, among others, some psychologists have stressed the importance of *mastery learning* (Block, 1971, Bloom, 1976).

In mastery learning stress is placed on ensuring that almost all students do master what is taught. In many classrooms this does not happen, largely because of practical difficulties arising from the fact that students differ from each other in the ease with which they learn and in the time they take to learn new materials. Consequently, the teacher moves on to further learning tasks well before some of the students have completely mastered the previous one.

Teachers who follow mastery-learning techniques deal with the classroom problems that individual differences cause by allowing slow learners more time to complete a learning task than individuals who learn quickly. This helps to ensure that, whilst there are inevitable differences between students in the total amount they learn, differences in the thoroughness with which materials have been learned are minimized. A policy such as this makes good sense when we consider the cumulative aspects of learning. Since what is learned at any one time is strongly influenced by existing knowledge and previously acquired skills, the student who can draw upon abilities that have been learned thoroughly will be better placed than someone whose previous learning experiences have resulted in an arrray, albeit possibly larger, of half-learned (and therefore easily forgotten) information.

Transfer of Learning

In the present book we shall return repeatedly to questions concerning the ways in which something that was learned at one time will influence future performance and future learning. This matter has been of longstanding interest to educators and to psychologists. In referring to it they have used the terms *transfer of learning* and *transfer of training*, drawing attention to the importance of knowing about the generalization or transfer of learning to new and different situations.

It could be argued that any learning has the potential of affecting the individuals's future performance in some circumstance or other, and therefore it is true in a sense that all learning transfers. However, in practical circumstances, there exist large differences in the extent to which different instances of learning generalize and are widely applicable. Teachers rightly give special attention to those intellectual skills and those kinds of knowledge which can contribute to a variety of useful achievements.

Two distinct kinds of question need to be asked about the transfer of learned abilities. The most obviously important questions ask about the extent to which something that was learned on one occasion *can be applied* to other tasks and other circumstances. The second kind of question, which educators sometimes forget to ask, concerns the extent to which a learner *will actually apply* (in different circumstances) knowledge and skills that appear (to mature and educated people) to be broadly applicable, or 'transferable'.

It is important to realize that having a positive answer to the first type of question does not always mean that an affirmative answer to questions of the second kind is justified. All too often, a child learns something which, so far as the teacher is concerned, is readily and easily applicable to other situations, but the child fails to apply what has been learned. Young and immature students do not spontaneously transfer learning to new and different tasks: they have to learn to do so. Often, considerable help and encouragement from the teacher is needed before a student will start to make use of a new skill in any circumstances that are at all different from those in which it was first acquired. The habit of applying learned abilities widely and imaginatively is not gained without experience and assistance.

Learning how to Learn

Among the abilities that transfer most widely are the skills that contribute to learning how to learn. No educational objective is more important for students than learning how to learn, and how to function as an independent, autonomous learner. The value of the various skills that can help a student to learn how to learn more effectively is stressed throughout this book.

Although much of what is learned at school takes the form of particular information or particular abilities that enable a person to cope with the demands of modern living, it is equally important for the school to equip a pupil to be able to go on learning after school, as our changing and complex world demands. Essentially, the school learner needs to have acquired a range of abilities necessary for further learning. A person who leaves school ill-equipped with competencies required for learning independently throughout the remainder of life is at a severe disadvantage.

Some emphasis on the acquisition of independent learning skills is evident in many curriculum materials and teachers' classroom activities. The teaching of numeracy and literacy is specifically designed to extend the range of circumstances in which a student can gain new knowledge and extended abilities. In recent years there has been a tendency for educators to give increased prominence to the goal of helping pupils to acquire expertise as independent learners. The findings of research into the psychology of learning confirm the value of this trend.

Introduction

In some respects, learning is not unlike other skilled crafts. To be successful, it is essential to gain the skills of the craft and to discover how to use the 'tools of the trade' in question. For learning, many of the tools of the trade take the form of learning strategies and techniques. The good learner has acquired a large repertoire of such techniques, and knows how to use them effectively, how to choose the most appropriate technique for a particular task, when to apply particular methods and how to adapt them for new uses.

There now exists a large body of evidence demonstrating the centrality of learners' processing activities and strategies in the acquisition of knowledge and abilities. This research has made possible some valuable advances in our knowledge of how students can learn to learn more effectively and independently. In the following chapters attention is given to methods and procedures that help individuals to gain skills than they can call upon for independent learning.

The Familiarity of Learning

Cast your mind back to the teachers' conversation at the beginning of the chapter. I remarked then that whatever we might think of the quality of the views expressed, there was clearly no shortage of ideas. This fact reminds us, as we begin to examine research into the psychological processes which lead to school learning, that the topic of human learning is not one that is at all esoteric or unfamiliar. Quite the reverse: for almost everyone, in and out of school, experiences of learning are extremely common. It is therefore not at all surprising that many people, like Charlie's teachers, have definite ideas about the factors that influence learning. Learning is a highly familiar part of our lives. Nothing characterizes the human species more completely than its dependence upon learning, and the existence of a person who lacks any ability to learn is hard to imagine.

The fact that learning is so familiar inevitably influences our approach to it as a topic of study. Usually, part of the difficulty that is experienced when we begin to study a new field of knowledge is due to the strangeness and unfamiliarity of the subject-matter and the ideas that have to be mastered. In the physical sciences, for example, technical vocabularies of terms and concepts need to be acquired. In studying learning, however, the familiarity of the topic ensures that there are fewer difficulties of this kind.

But the very familiarity of learning can introduce problems that hinder our attempts to understand it. The fact that as adult humans we are such highly experienced learners, experts perhaps, undoubtedly provides us with knowledge that can make a valuable contribution to the investigation of learning. But the same familiarity may also lead to our having some rigid ideas about learning. These can take the form of beliefs, attitudes and prejudices that can make it difficult for us to examine learning in the objective and dispassionate manner that is associated with scientific enquiry and that is necessary in order to gain deeper understanding.

In studying human learning we should make good use of our own knowledge and experience, but it is also essential to guard against being blinkered by our preconceptions. For example, because it may seem 'obvious' that learning and remembering are entirely different, it may be hard to understand that they may be controlled by largely identical mechanisms. As was noted earlier, whilst in everyday life it may often be useful to distinguish between learning and memory, making such a distinction is not necessarily so helpful when we are attempting to understand the factors that lead to students acquiring abilities gained at school. Again, it may seem equally 'obvious' to us that our mental activities, including learning, are largely controlled by conscious processes. In fact this is not so. Conscious minds have only a very limited knowledge of the workings of the brain's cognitive computing processes that are responsible for human learning.

There is another way in which our thinking about human learning is influenced by its familiarity and importance in everyday life. Partly because learning is so crucial to us, we sometimes find it hard to distinguish between those kinds of questions which psychological research can legitimately aim to answer, relating to the causes, explanation and prediction of learning, and certain broader, value-laden questions, such as 'What *should* a child learn at school?'; 'Is it the job of the school to teach driving?', 'Should students at school be encouraged to question the values of their society?' and so on. It might seem that the two types of question are quite distinct, and that in studying the psychology of learning we can concentrate on the former and ignore the latter. In practice, it is not always easy to do this.

Of course, there is no harm in psychologists expressing their own opinions concerning any aspect of learning. On matters concerning the explanation and understanding of learning phenomena the psychologist can speak with the authority that scientific expertise and objective approaches to investigation make possible. It is important to realize, however, that the same authority cannot be claimed when the views expressed concern issues that are matters for educational, political or ethical debate, rather than ones that can be decided on the basis of scientific knowledge alone.

2

The Importance of Mental Activities

Introduction

The mental activities of individual students form a powerful source of influence on what is actually learned. This chapter introduces some psychological research investigating the effects of learners' mental processing activities. Later, in chapter 3, we shall examine a wider range of students' mental activities and strategies, including ones that play crucial roles in classroom learning.

In a simple experiment, psychologists asked some students to spend one minute looking at a coloured picture. It showed a living room, and was taken from a magazine. Afterwards, everyone was asked to recall the items they had seen in the picture. Despite the fact that all the participants had looked at the identical picture for exactly the same amount of time, the recall test findings showed that some people retained over ten times as much information as others about the items depicted in the picture.

What was the cause of this huge difference in the amount that different people learned? The reason cannot lie in conditions of presenting the information or in the time that was available, since these factors were identical for all the students. From a teacher's point of view, it would be especially interesting to know whether the differences in learning were caused by events that can be manipulated in the classroom, such as the instructions to the students, or whether the reasons for the differences were factors that a teacher cannot so readily control, such as the abilities of the people who participated in the experiment. If the former alternative is correct, exactly what were the causes of the differences in the students' performance? All teachers stand to gain from knowing about factors that can exert such a strong influence on human learning.

In fact, the participants in the experiment (by Bransford, Nitsch and Franks, 1977) had been divided into four groups. In two of the groups students were told that within the picture up to three very small *x*s had been inked in. The participants in Group One were instructed to look for the *x*s, by scanning the picture vertically and horizontally. They were also told that they would be asked to say how many *x*s they had located. Group Two subjects were told that the *x*s would appear on the contours of objects within the picture. Therefore, they should direct their attention to the contours. In actuality, however, the pictures in neither condition contained any inked-in *x*s at all.

There were two further conditions in the experiment. The students in Group Three were told to look at the picture of the living-room and think of actions which they might perform on the objects they saw there. Group Four participants were told that after the picture was taken away they would be required to form a visual image of it. Both these sets of instructions encouraged the students to learn about the contents of the picture.

The students' recall-test scores showed that the subjects in Groups Three and Four retained considerably more information than the other students. In Groups One and Two between three and eight items were recalled. Recall by participants in the third and fourth groups was considerably higher: they ranged from 25 to 32 objects. To say the least, this represents a very large improvement over performance in the other conditions.

The findings of this experiment show that when people are exposed to visual information, the extent to which they learn from looking at it is by no means determined solely by external factors such as the way in which the information is displayed, or by the amount of time available to study. At least equally important are the mental activities that people undertake as they attend to and perceive the material that is presented to them. For this reason, a knowledge about the ways in which children's mental activities influence learning and remembering, and an understanding of the kinds of mental activities that are associated with success in classroom learning circumstances, can be of immense value to the teacher.

Stages in learning and memory

In this chapter and the next we shall be examining various kinds of mental activities that learners undertake, noting how each kind of activity contributes to learning. Broadly speaking, activities can have an influence at three essential stages in the acquisition of learned knowledge and skills. First, there is an *input* stage, at which items or events are perceived. As is clear from the experiment described above, the nature of the mental processing that takes place at this stage, when items are first perceived, crucially affects the learning outcome. Next, the processed information is *retained* by the brain's 'long-term memory', And since the amount of information that any person has to retain is vast, the human brain needs to have sophisticated mechanisms for ensuring that information is retained securely and in a manner that makes it possible for particular items to be quickly located when they are needed.

Locating information that is already retained in the brain constitutes the third essential stage, *retrieval*. The data that are retrieved from memory can take many different forms, including knowledge, skills, simple and complex concepts, and rules. The ease with which a stored item of information can be located depends partly upon the mental activities that occurred prior to retrieval (which determine how an item of information is stored within the body of knowledge retained in a person's brain) and partly upon activities that take place at the time of retrieval. Later, we shall examine how retrieval plans – the mental processes and the strategies by which an individual attempts to locate information that is retained in memory – help determine whether stored items are actually accessible to the learner. However impressive is the quantity and variety of information stored in a person's brain, unless it can be readily retrieved it remains unavailable to the individual, and is of no real value.

In classroom learning, various practical questions concerning the retrievability of stored knowledge and skills have further importance because they affect the transferability of what has been learned. Sometimes, teachers err on the side of optimism by assuming that a young student will readily be able to transfer or apply newly learned skills to situations that are very different from the circumstances in which the skills were acquired. Knowing about the retrieval stage in memory and learning helps us to understand how transfer of knowledge and skills can be maximized.

Psychological experiments and classroom learning

Teachers have to be especially concerned with those kinds of learning that are important for the child at school: many of the experiments that are described in this book were conducted either in schools or in school-like circumstances. However, in everyday school-life the various different factors which influence learning tend to operate together, simultaneously. In order to make scientific progress despite this complexity, and gain an understanding of the separate effects of each of the many influencing factors, it is often necessary to design experiments in which the normal conditions of day-to-day learning are artificially simplified. Such an 'analytic' approach is necessary in most spheres of scientific activity, in order to make progress towards understanding highly complex, multiply-determined phenomena.

Consequently, in much of the experimental research that has been conducted by psychologists to investigate learning, the circumstances in which learning occurs are simpler or more straightforward than is customary in real life. Obviously, the relevance to real life of any experimental findings that were obtained in a simplified or artifical situation is questionable. In order to ensure maximum relevance, such research needs to be followed up by studies undertaken under more realistic conditions. But it is worth stressing that there are often good reasons for psychologists deciding to conduct experiments in which some of the complexities of everyday school learning are reduced. For example, many of the experiments described in the present chapter involved learning very simple materials. These were chosen partly in order for it to be possible to examine the effects on learning of students' activities while excluding other influences on learning, such as those of the learner's existing knowledge, that are normally present in school learning situations.

We must not forget that all learners are individuals. In real life the unique past experience of every learner is a major influence. One implication of this fact is that, so far as individual learners are concerned, there are inevitable limitations on the validity of generalizations that are based on the *average* performances by participants in experimental research. Research findings can rarely predict precisely what a particular individual will do.

Processing Perceived Visual Events

The mental activities to be considered next are ones that take place at the *input* or perceptual stage. These activities do not necessarily involve the individual making any deliberate attempt to learn. Later, we shall examine some activities which definitely do reflect a person's conscious effort to learn or remember.

The experiment described at the beginning of the chapter has illustrated the large influence exerted by the processing activities that occur when a person first perceives visual materials. One might be tempted to conclude that the findings merely demonstrate that people learn most efficiently when attention is directed to the meaningful aspects of what is perceived. There is some truth in this suggestion: attending to the most meaningful aspects of what is perceived undoubtedly contributes to meaningful learning. However, it over-simplifies the relationship between learning and perceptual (input) processing, as the findings of another experiment demonstrate. In this study, conducted by G. H. Bower and M. B. Karlin (1974), people looked at pictures of unfamiliar faces. Some of the participants were simply told to note whether each face was male or female. The other participants had to rate the faces in terms of the degree to which they thought them to be likeable, and also according to judgements of the honesty of the faces. Note that in this study, unlike the one described earlier, all the subjects had to attend to the *meaning* of the materials. However, rating faces in terms of likeableness and honesty probably required more extensive mental processing than was necessary for simply classifying faces on the basis of sex.

The main finding was that memory for the faces (measured by a test of recognition) was considerably better among those participants who had to rank the faces' personality attributes rather than simply deciding on their sex. As in the previous experiment, the conditions of presentation were identical in the two conditions: all the subjects saw exactly the same faces for equivalent periods of time. Therefore, the differences in learning must have been caused by the subjects who participated in the two conditions of the experiment *acting differently* in some respect. Presumably, the alternative instructions led to different input processing activities occurring when the unfamiliar faces were perceived. We might say that the students who rated likeableness and honesty had to do more (mental) work than the other subjects, as they inspected the faces.

Processing and Learning Language-based Materials

At school, a large proportion of the learning that takes place involves language and the written word. With language-based materials, do learners' perceptual processing activities exert similar effects to the ones we have observed with pictorial information? Evidence from further experiments has established that the answer to this question is a definite 'Yes'.

In a study conducted by Fergus Craik and Endel Tulving (1975), college students who were enrolled in a course on learning and memory were given booklets containing a number of questions. They were told that each question would ask them about a word that they were going to see. The word was then projected for one second on a screen at the front of the room. After seeing the word, subjects wrote down the answer to the question. For example, the question might say, 'Does it rhyme with STONE?' If the word that subsequently appeared was BONE the subject would write an affirmative answer.

There were three types of question. Some questions asked about the *meaningful* (or *semantic*) category of the word that was about to be seen (e.g. 'Is it an animal?'). Other questions asked about the *sound* of the word (e.g. 'Does it rhyme with LEMON?'). Questions of the third kind asked about the visual format or *type case* in which the word was to appear (e.g. 'Is it in capital letters?'). The correct answer was 'Yes' and 'No' with equal frequency.

The student participants each answered 60 questions, 20 of each kind, randomly ordered. Afterwards they were given a surprise test to measure their retention of the 60 words. The test consisted of a list containing 180 words in all. Participants were told that 60 of these items were the ones which they had already seen. Their task was to identify the words that were recognized.

The experimenters wanted to discover whether the different kinds of mental processing activities that participants undertook in order to answer the three kinds of questions would have any influence on the students' retention of the words, as measured by a recognition test. All the words had been displayed for an identical period of time, and exactly the same words were used in the different experimental conditions. (This was achieved by, for example, coupling the same word with a question about its meaning for some participants, and with a question about its sound for others.) Therefore, to find the cause of any differences in recognition-test scores we would need to look at the participants and their own activities rather than the conditions under which the materials were presented.

The percentages of words recognized following the different kinds of questions are shown below.

Visual structure (type-case)	26%
Sound (rhyme)	46%
Meaningful category	72%

It is clear from these findings that the input processing which takes place when someone perceives a word has a very substantial influence upon the probability of that word being subsequently recognized. As in the other experiments, there were very substantial differences between the conditions in the amounts of information that the students retained, despite the fact that in each condition the same words were displayed for an identical length of time.

Interpreting the findings

These findings are undoubtedly striking, but perhaps we should be more cautious in interpreting them. Is it inevitable that they reflect differences in perceptual processing at the input stage? One conceivable alternative explanation is that following the different kinds of question, subjects spend different amounts of time actually attending to the word they see. The findings also raise certain other queries. For example, if, as the results show, questions about the meaning of a word lead to better remembering than other kinds of questions, does it follow that all questions about meanings of items are equally effective, or do some meaningful questions lead to better recall than others?

Another matter of uncertainty is that of the importance of making an effort to learn. In the above experiment the participants were not told to expect a recognition test, but some of them might have guessed that one would follow. It would be interesting to know how the experimental results would have been affected, if at all, if all the participants had been making a deliberate effort to learn. Again, in the present experiment there does not seem to have been much incentive for subjects to perform well in the recognition test, whereas in many school tasks there are strong incentives to learn. Would incentives to do well have influenced the results of the study?

Issues arising from input processing studies

In order to clarify some of these additional issues the authors carried out a number of further experiments, totalling ten in all. In most of the experiments, unlike the one already described, the subjects were tested individually rather than in a group. With individual testing it was possible to exert more precise control over details of the procedure, and subjects' responses could be accurately timed. The period of time for which the words was presented was one-fifth of a second. Participants responded to each question ('Is it a —?') by pressing one of two keys, marked 'YES' and 'NO', as quickly as possible.

Sentence complexity. One outcome of having more precise experimental control over the presentation and timing of the materials was to accentuate the effects of having different kinds of questions. In every experiment subjects remembered at least twice as many of the words that were preceded by questions that asked about meanings as the other words: in one study participants retained as much as thirteen times the number of items. Another finding was that the particular form of the meaningful questions was important. The questions in one experiment required subjects to state whether the word that was about to be seen would fit into a given sentence. It was found that when the preceding sentence was relatively complex (e.g. 'The small lady angrily picked up the red —') there was a higher probability that the word would subsequently be recalled than when the sentence was of medium complexity ('The ripe — tasted delicious') or was simple ('The — is torn'). Assuming that it is correct to say that the mental processing required for the decision task is related to the complexity of the sentence, these findings indicate that memory for meaningfully perceived items is related to the extensiveness of the processing they undergo.

It has been suggested that the *depth* of mental processing is the crucial factor (Craik and Lockhart, 1972). However, this creates some problems: for example, it is not entirely clear how 'deep' processing differs from 'shallow' processing, or how the depth of processing can be measured directly.

Adding to the complexity of sentences is not the only way to increase the meaningfulness of tasks. Another important influence resides in the extent to which information has *personal relevance* to the individual. The possibility that events which have personal importance may be especially well processed was examined by another research group (Rogers, Kuiper and Kirker, 1977). The design of their study was similar to those we have described, but as an added feature there was a fourth, 'self-reference', condition in which the questions that preceded a word asked whether the item (which was always an adjective, for instance *happy*, *mean* or *miserable*) was one which described the individual participant.

Subsequently, there was a recall test. As in the experiments reported by Craik and Tulving, it was found that words preceded by questions that asked about their meaning (by enquiring whether the word meant the same as another word) were recalled more frequently than words preceded by questions about their physical structure, by a factor of about three to one. But recall of the words preceded by a self-reference question ('Describes you?') was even better: subjects' recall of these items was nearly twice as good as it was for words that followed an ordinary question about the meaning ('Means the same as —?').

Time as a possible influence. A further experiment was designed to examine the possibility that the observed relationship between learning and the kinds of questions that participants had to answer was simply due to more *time* being taken to answer those questions that necessitated taking account of word meanings. In the first of the experiments, although all the words were presented for the same amount of time (one second) it is conceivable that the time for which participants actually attended to them might have varied systematically, according to the form of the prior question. Furthermore, in some of those studies in which subjects were tested individually and their response times to answer the questions were measured, the experimenters observed that questions referring to the meanings of items took longer to answer than questions about the words' sound or visual appearance. Therefore, variations in the time spent in mental processing cannot be ruled out as an alternative explanation of the differences in retention.

To clarify this matter a further study was undertaken, in which the questions about aspects of the words other than their meanings were carefully designed to ensure that answering them would take just as long a time as answering questions about the meanings of words. This was achieved by requiring subjects to state whether or not a word had a particular consonant–vowel (C–V) pattern. For example, the question might ask whether the following item fitted the pattern CCVVC. If the word was, say, BRAIN the correct answer was 'Yes'. The average response time to reply to questions like these was 1.7 seconds, roughly twice the response time for questions about the meanings of words ('Is it a —?'). Nevertheless, words preceded by questions of the latter form were better remembered. We can therefore rule out the possibility that the earlier result was due solely to differences in the time taken for the question-answering task.

Effects of intentions and incentives. A further experiment in the series conducted by Craik and Tulving casts light on the effects of *having a definite intention to learn*. In some of their experiments, but not others, subjects knew in advance that retention would be tested. Perhaps surprisingly, this seemed to make little or no difference to the results.

Another good way to ensure that individuals have a definite intention to learn is to give them a strong incentive: one experiment was designed to assess the effects of systematically varying the incentives. Students were told in advance that they would be rewarded with one, three or six cents for every word they recognized correctly. As in the previous experiments, there were different kinds of questions. Thus it was possible to compare the effects on word recognition of (1) the type of task and (2) the level of reward.

There was a very clear result. The effects of the type of question were similar to those observed in the other experiments, but varying the reward level had no effect at all. This finding indicates that differences in intention to learn or remember were not an important factor in the present series of experiments. That is not to say that incentives and intentions have no effect in everyday learning. However, the present results do indicate that their effects are *indirect*. Incentives affect everyday learning either by raising the probability that an individual will attend, or by encouraging a person to engage in extensive processing of the items to be learned. But when attention and processing are tightly controlled, as in the present series of experiments, any effects of incentives are eliminated. This shows that incentives and intentions have no *direct* influence on learning.

Some conclusions

The experiments that have been described in the present chapter provide firm evidence that people's active mental processing operations are important causes of learning and remembering. The experimental procedure is admittedly artificial and different from the usual circumstances of school learning, but it has the great advantage of making it possible to control or eliminate all of the possible influences other than those introduced by the individual learner. Consequently, it is possible to state without any doubt that factors *within the learner* are responsible for the large and striking effects that were observed.

In all of the above studies the method used for manipulating subjects' mental activities involved asking questions concerning words that were about to be seen. Input processing can also be manipulated in other ways, such as by requiring participants to rate items on the basis of the perceived importance or pleasantness, detecting particular letters, and counting syllables (Hyde and Jenkins, 1969). The results of studies using tasks such as these have been substantially similar to the findings that have been described in this chapter.

Processing Activities and Young Children's Learning

The term *elaboration* has been introduced to describe those activities in which learners use any of the strategies that involve acting upon and 'elaborating' the items to be learned, for example by connecting them or relating them to other materials, or generating an image of them. As children get older they adopt elaborative strategies increasingly frequently.

The effectiveness of elaborative strategies for helping young children to learn is dramaticaly illustrated in a study by Turnure, Buium and Thurlow (1976). The five-year-old subjects in this study looked at illustrations, each of which depicted a pair of familiar objects. There were a number of different conditions, but in all of them the same pictures were presented for an identical period of time. As in the previous studies, the only factor that differed between the conditions was the mental activity of the subjects. The experimenters were interested in observing the effects of this activity upon the children's recall of the objects.

Some of the children were told simply to name the objects they saw. Others were told to make up a sentence that joined together the words denoting each of the two objects. For example, for a picture of a piece of soap and a jacket, a suitable linking sentence would be 'The soap is hiding in the jacket'. One group of children made up their own sentences; other children simply repeated sentences that the experimenter provided for them. Children in a further experimental condition were asked questions that required them to think about possible relationships of the two objects depicted. For example, typical questions were 'What is the soap doing under the jacket?' and 'Why is the soap in the jacket?'

Each child worked through 21 such pairs of pictured objects. Next there followed a surprise recall test, in which one item from each pair was shown and the child was asked to recall the object that went with it. From our knowledge of the experiments previously described we would expect the different tasks given to the children to lead to differences in recall. This did happen in the present study. What is more surprising, however, is the sheer size of the variations in recall between the different conditions. Those children who were required simply to provide the words for the objects presented to them recalled, on average, only one out of the twenty-one items. The children who produced joining sentences did somewhat better: those who repeated sentences which the experimenter had provided recalled an average of three items, and average recall by the children who made up their own linking sentences was eight items. But the child participants who answered questions about each pair of items did even better than that. They recalled, on average, as many as 16 out of the 21 items.

In short, despite the fact that exactly the same items were presented in the different conditions of the experiment, for identical periods of time, there were quite enormous differences in what the young children actually learned. As in the other studies, it is clear that the cause of such differences lay in the different mental-processing activities demanded by the various tasks. We might note that the procedure in which children asked questions about the items provided a particularly effective method of helping children to learn, and one that could readily be adapted for use in school classrooms.

Can young children be trained to use the highly successful interrogative strategy by asking questions for themselves? A study designed to investigate this found that it is certainly possible even in children as young as four years of age. Young children taught to ask themselves questions similar to those used in the investigation by Turnure, Buium and Thurlow were able to recall three times as many items as untrained children, and they maintained their use of the strategy over a long period, without prompting, and they were able to transfer the skill to different learning tasks.

A concluding remark

From the evidence described in this chapter it is abundantly clear that students' own activities form a key factor determining learning. At school, the activities that produce learning are typically more complicated and they are often deliberately introduced with learning in mind. As children get older they become increasingly adept at using plans and strategies in which their mental activities are organized in ways that are effective for promoting learning. In the next chapter we shall examine some of those activities by students that are necessary for classroom learning.

3

Activities, Strategies and School Learning

Rehearsal

Most of the mental activities that learners carried out in the experiments described in the previous chapter were ones that individuals performed, knowingly or otherwise, without having a deliberate intent to learn. We now turn to actions that do reflect a student's conscious efforts to learn. Learning to learn is largely a matter of learning what to do in order to be a successful learner. First, we shall consider *rehearsal*.

Rehearsal is probably the most widespread of all the deliberate strategies used by young students in order to help them acquire knowledge and skills. Rehearsal is useful for many of the learning tasks that are encountered at school, and most children who have been attending school for several years habitually rehearse when it is appropriate to do so. Nevertheless, the strategy of rehearsing does have to be acquired: it is a learned skill, and one which many young children do not possess.

Research has been undertaken to discover whether young children who do not spontaneously rehearse can be taught to do so. If a newly acquired ability to rehearse is widely effective in increasing a pupil's success at school learning, gaining useful rehearsal skills can be regarded as an early instance of the child's learning how to learn.

Detecting rehearsal and measuring its effects

In order to investigate rehearsal scientifically, psychologists first had to solve the practical problem of detecting whether an individual is rehearsing or not. We can simply ask a child if he is rehearsing, of course, but people's subjective reports about their own mental activities are notoriously unreliable, especially in young children. Fortunately, there is a more direct way of measuring rehearsal in children. It so happens that young children, unlike adults, often move their lips as they rehearse. consequently, by observing lip movements we can gain a fairly accurate indication of a child's rehearsal activities.

In one study of children's rehearsal, John Flavell and his co-researchers (Flavell, Beach and Chinsky, 1966) observed lip movements as children looked at common objects that they had been told to remember. Among the older subjects, who were aged ten years, seventeen out of the twenty children observed were seen to be moving their lips. But amongst the youngest children, aged five, lip movements were seen in only two subjects out of twenty. Predictably, it was found that the older subjects remembered more objects than the younger ones, but the investigators also observed that at each age those children who moved their lips recalled more items than those who did not move their lips.

Training non-rehearsers to rehearse

The above result is strongly consistent with the view that rehearsal made a positive contribution to performance at the task. Confirmatory evidence for this assertion would be provided if it was discovered that when the children who did *not* rehearse were taught to do so they would remember more of the items. To investigate this, some six- and seven-year-olds who did not spontaneously rehearse were carefully taught how to do so. They were told to whisper the names of the objects they were looking at until the moment when they were instructed to begin recall. (Interestingly, the children did not find it difficult to follow the rehearsal instructions. Children of this age seem to acquire the strategy of rehearsing fairly easily, if they are properly taught.) The outcome of teaching the children to rehearse was to improve their remembering considerably, to the extent that their success at recalling information reached the levels achieved by those children of the same age who rehearsed spontaneously.

It is valuable for children at school to be able to rehearse. It is surprising to find that, even by ten years of age, not all children rehearse spontaneously in circumstances where doing so would be clearly advantageous. Why is this so? A possible reason is that because it is such a widespread and apparently easy-to-use strategy, teachers and other adults take it for granted, wrongly, that all children do know how to rehearse and appreciate the value of doing so.

Some children are taught how to rehearse by a parent or a teacher, others may acquire the skill through imitating another child rehearsing, perhaps a brother or sister, and some children discover for themselves that repeating words makes them easier to recall. But there are other young children who fall into none of these categories: they fail to acquire this useful skill. For these pupils, explicit instruction in how-to-rehearse by the classroom teacher can make a very real contribution towards learning how to learn.

Making use of rehearsal skills

Although it may be easy for a child to learn to rehearse, it would be wrong to assume that once the strategy has been acquired a child will make use of it whenever circumstances arrive in which rehearsing can be useful. To gain the maximum advantages of any learning strategy the individual must not only learn to use the strategy but he must also acquire the *habit* of doing so, and also gain practice in *applying* the strategy in circumstances that differ from those in which it was initially acquired. Learning how to learn effectively is not just a matter of acquiring particular techniques and strategies. Teachers need to be equally concerned with helping pupils get into the habit of using and applying them.

We noted in chapter 1 that immature individuals do not necessarily take full advantage of newly gained skills unless they are given encouragement and opportunities to practise. Rehearsal does not transfer automatically. Young children need to gain sufficient experience of using a new skill for it to become a habit: they have to acquire confidence in using techniques that are initially unfamiliar. When faced with tasks that are strange, many people, and children especially, are prone to fall back to using those procedures that are familiar, tried and tested, even when it would seem obvious to a more experienced learner that a recently acquired learning strategy would be much more effective.

Rehearsal can take many forms. The student at school uses rehearsal in order to help remember information that must be learned. Typically, sentence-length passages will be rehearsed, rather than single words. Sometimes it will be necessary for a student to memorize materials verbatim, or word for word, for example when a poem or a speech has to be learned. More often, only the sense or gist needs to be learned. The particular form of a good rehearsal strategy will depend upon the detailed nature of the task.

The effects of recitation

One interesting study investigating the effects of rehearsal on the acquisition of prose knowledge was published early in the present century (Gates, 1917). Gates designed a number of experiments to examine the effects of telling students who were learning from prose passages which they read to rehearse the content they were attempting to learn. The ages of the subjects ranged from nine to fourteen years. They read highly meaningful passages in the form of biographies. Gates told the subjects to rehearse the materials by looking away from the passage and saying the contents to themselves.

At all ages the participants learned better when a substantial part of their study time was devoted to rehearsal than when the whole period was spent in reading. On the whole, the most successful procedure was to spend about 40 per cent of the time reading, with the remaining 60 per cent allotted to rehearsal. In these circumstances students' retention of the biographical information improved by around 30 per cent, on average, compared with the condition in which they spent the whole study period simply reading. For the younger children, aged nine years, the advantage of combining reading and rehearsal over reading alone was greater, averaging 36 per cent. For the oldest students, aged around 14 years, there was a smaller advantage, of around 18 per cent. Note that this is nonetheless a marked improvement.

The optimum proportion of the study time to be devoted to rehearsal depended upon the age of the learners. For the older children learning was at least as good when 80 per cent of the time was spent rehearsing as when rehearsal occupied 60 per cent of the total study time. With the younger subjects, however, devoting more than 60 per cent of the time to rehearsal led to decreased learning scores.

Self-testing

Related to rehearsal and recitation are a number of broadly similar study activities, including self-testing and answering a teacher's questions about prose materials that are being learned. Numerous studies have been undertaken in order to investigate the effects of inserting questions into prose materials, and many experiments have examined the outcomes of using testing students.

On the whole, the research findings are in line with commonsense predictions. Testing does have beneficial effects, their form and magnitude largely depending on the particular circumstances. Similarly, inserting questions into text usually aids learning. In some studies the exact form of the improvements in learning has been found to depend, not surprisingly, upon the type of questions used and their position in the text.

An experiment by Duchastel (1982) provides a good example of recent research into the effects of testing on school learning. American high-school students read a 1700-word passage containing 12 paragraphs that each described a topic of British history during the reign of Queen Victoria. After reading the prose text some of the students were immediately given a test on the contents of the passage. Some other students, who formed a control group, spent an equivalent amount of time completing a study habits questionnaire.

Two weeks later all the students were tested for long-term retention of the passage contents. On this occasion those participants who had been tested immediately after reading the passage were found to have retained the material much more successfully than the other students. The tested individuals recalled no less than twice as many items as the subjects who were in the control group.

In this experiment we can rule out the possibility that the improvement was solely due to some participants becoming familiar with particular test questions, since those participants who were given multiple-choice questions in the immediate test and short-answer questions in the long-term test administered two weeks later (or *vice versa*) performed almost as well as subjects who received the same form of test on both occasions.

Organizing

Another way in which students' mental activities contribute to
learning is through organizing new information. People find it hard
to retain information when it takes the form of a large number of
separate and unrelated items. Furthermore, information that is
stored in a well-organized manner is generally more easy to retrieve
when the learner needs to recall it. Remembering will usually be
increased by any procedure that helps the learner to form connections between such materials, or to form connections between new
to-be-learned items and the individual's existing knowledge.

The arbitrariness of the distinction between the effects of a
learner's activities and the influence of the same individual's knowledge is especially apparent when organizational activities are
described, since the manner in which a person undertakes the
mental activities responsible for organizing information largely
depends upon that person's state of knowledge.

Using a narrative strategy

The influence of a student's organizing activities upon learning and
remembering is most clearly illustrated by studies using materials
that are presented to the learner in a completely unconnected form.
The college students who participated in one experiment (Bower
and Clark, 1969) learned twelve lists of words, each containing ten
nouns representing concrete items. Some of the subjects studied
each list for 90 seconds, and afterwards wrote down the words they
could recall. Most participants found this quite easy and were able
to remember the majority of the words.

After they had worked through all twelve lists, the subjects were
asked to recall as many as possible of all the words they had
studied, the total being 120 (ten items in each of twelve lists). At
this stage those participants who had received no instruction in a
learning strategy found it impossible to recall more than a small
proportion of the 120 words: average correct recall by these
students was less than 20 per cent.

The performance of another group of students was very much
better. These students had participated under identical conditions,
with the same word lists and similar presentation times, but with

one difference. They had been instructed to adopt a particular strategy as they studied the lists of words. They were told to try to form a *narrative* that would connect all ten words in each list. Some practice lists were provided, so that the students had the opportunity to gain some experience in forming narratives. After a couple of such practice trials all the students found it fairly easy to do so.

The following is a typical example of a narrative: it was produced by one of the participants. The ten words that appeared on the list originally presented to the student are shown in italics.

> A *vegetable* can be a useful *instrument* for a *college* student. A *carrot* can be a *nail* for your fence or *basin*. But a *merchant* of the *Queen* would *scale* the fence and feed the carrot to a *goat*.

During the experiment those students who had been instructed to use the narrative organizing strategy did not perform any better than the other students at the tests measuring immediate recall of each list. Thus the narrative strategy did not at first appear to have any beneficial effects. However, after all 12 lists had been studied, when the students were asked to recall as many as possible of all the words they had seen, those who had followed the narrative strategy performed very much better than the others. As has been mentioned, the other students recalled less than 20 per cent of the words, at this stage. However, the students who had been instructed to use the narrative strategy recalled, on average, more than 90 per cent of the words.

This result demonstrates that a mental strategy that involves learners organizing the information they perceive can have a huge influence upon remembering. Moreover, the effect demonstrated in the present study is a highly robust one: the present author has repeated the experiment several times with groups of students, always with the same findings. It is true that the word lists learned in the study comprise items of information that are more completely separate and isolated from one another than is usually found in the materials encountered in school learning. Since most of the information that a student learns at school is already organized to some extent, it is unlikely that everyday organizational activities by a learner can exert quite such a large influence as the 400 per cent improvement that occurred in this study. However, providing that the manner in which information is presented to a student leaves at least *some* room for the student to undertake mental organizing activities, definite increases in learning can be expected.

Other organizing activities

Organizational activities that are based upon the sentence structure of writtten language are particularly effective, but alternative kinds of organization can also be useful. In general, any procedure that serves to link disconnected items is likely to aid learning. For example, in a number of experiments it has been found that recall of large numbers of separate items is improved when learners are encouraged to sort the items into groups or categories. On the whole, older children and adults are more likely to engage spontaneously in this kind of organizing activity than young children. People are much better at acquiring interrelated bodies of knowledge than remembering unconnected pieces of information, as is apparent from the difficulty that many students experience in trying to learn items of vocabulary in an unfamiliar foreign language.

The essential outcome of a learner's organizing activities is to reduce the number of entirely separate items that have to be remembered. This function is demonstrated in an investigation conducted by S. Smith (Miller, 1956). His aim was to increase his memory-span for sequences of the binary digits 0 and 1. He trained himself and a number of students to group the items in pairs and then *recode* them, substituting 0 for 00, 1 for 01, 2 for 10 and 3 for 11. In this way it was possible to halve the number of single digits in a sequence. For example, the 18-item list 101000100111001110 is reduced to 220213032, which is much easier to remember.

The normal memory span for random sequences of binary digits is around eight or nine items, but by recoding the digits Smith and his students were easily able to remember eighteen-item sequences. Moreover, by using more complicated systems of recoding, enabling three, four, or even 5 binary digits to be replaced by a single item Smith managed to increase his own memory span to as much as forty items.

A recoding system for organizing information appears to have a major disadvantage as a learning strategy. It seems to make an initially simple task (remembering a string of digits) into a much more cumbersome one. For example, in Smith's system it was necessary for him to recode the binary items at the time of input into a smaller number of digits, then retain the recoded sequence, and subsequently, in order to recall the list, decode the items back into the original binary digits.

As it happens, it is quite common to find that strategic methods and techniques designed to assist learning appear to make learning procedures more complicated. Intuitively, it seems that making a simple task into a more complicated one would reduce a person's performance, rather than increase it! The main reason why this does not happen is because the strategic procedures have the effect of transforming a task that involves a form of learning at which people perform rather badly into a task (albeit a more cumbersome one) which people can do well. Humans find it particularly difficult to remember large numbers of unrelated items of information. Reducing this source of difficulty in a learning task almost always makes it easier.

Using the system that Smith devised necessitates a certain amount of training, since the person using the methods has to be able to recode the items quickly and easily. Given sufficient training, highly complex recoding systems for increasing remembering can be acquired. With enough practice, people's ability to remember information about familiar items and events can increase dramatically. For instance, many waitresses in cocktail bars can remember vastly longer lists of drink orders than students can recall (Bennett, 1983).

Over a two-year period, one individual was able to increase his memory span for digits from about eight items to over two hundred items! This feat (described in a report by Chase and Ericsson, 1981) necessitated considerable practice, of course, and the man who performed it was aided by being able to draw upon an interest in competitive running. He could perceive many multi-item digit sequences as being running times, highly meaningful to him, for various competitive athletic events. He used his *knowledge* of running in order to undertake a mental organizing *activity*, in which sequences of unrelated digits were recoded as single running times. For this particular individual, it was a highly effective method of cutting down the number of functionally separate items to be remembered.

Imagery

In those learning strategies that make use of rehearsal and organizing activities the learner's manipulations of the information keep it within the language-based form in which it was presented. Imagery-based strategies are fundamentally different in this respect. Typically, the learner's activity involves some kind of *transformation* of the data to be learned from a verbal form into a representation that is essentially visual or pictorial.

Strategies that are based on visual imagery can be highly effective in some circumstances. They form a stock-in-trade of performers who display impressive memory feats, and they are strongly recommended by the writers of books and courses of instruction that claim to give their readers a 'Super-Power Memory'. Such 'memory experts' are sometimes called 'mnemonists'. The term 'mnemonic' simply means a memory-aid, although when people use it they are often (but not always) referring to those kinds of memory strategies in which visual imagery plays a crucial role.

In general, the function of strategies that use imagery is to provide a way of connecting a number of separate items that a person needs to remember. In this respect the role of imagery is not unlike that of a learner's mental organizing activities. However, whereas most of the other mental activities that are described in the present chapter have the additional function of helping to link the new information that is to be learned with the person's existing body of knowledge and skills, imagery does not do so to any great extent. In chapter 4 we shall discover the enormous significance for learning of the individual's being able to find ways to connect newly perceived information to existing knowledge and existing skills. The fact that imagery-based strategies do not, on the whole, contribute substantially towards forming linkages of this kind places a limitation on their value.

The keyword method and foreign-language acquisition

Nevertheless, imagery can be extremely useful to the learner. People differ in the ease with which they can form visual images (and some normal individuals are incapable of making images at all), but there are some learning tasks in which most people can benefit from using a strategy that requires them to form visual images. In foreign-language acquisition, for example, a mnemonic strategy that involves learners forming images can be very effective for helping students to acquire vocabulary items.

The technique is called the *keyword method* (Raugh and Atkinson, 1975; Pressley, 1977; Kasper, 1983). It provides a way of forming an easily remembered connection between a foreign-language word and its English equivalent. This is achieved by making two links. First, the student learns to link the foreign-language word with the keyword, which is an English word that is easily retained because it sounds similar to the foreign-language word being learned. Secondly, the learner is told to form a visual image in which the item denoted by the foreign word and the object denoted by the keyword are visualized together.

Imagine, for instance, that a student learning Russian wants to remember the word *zvonok* (pronounced, roughly 'zvan-oak'), which means *bell*. Initially, a keyword is formed. In this case a suitable keyword is *oak*. It is quite easy to learn the connection between *zvonok* and the similar-sounding word *oak*. Next, the second link is established, between the keyword (*oak*) and the English equivalent (*bell*) of the foreign word. This is the stage at which an image is formed by the learner. In this example the student might make a strong visual image in which a large bell is seen to be hanging from an oak tree.

Having formed these two easily learned links, the student has effectively made a learned connection between the foreign word and its English equivalent. The method can be used with any language, so long as appropriate keywords can be devised. In selecting keywords, an effort is made to find items which sound as similar as possible to the foreign word and to ensure that each keyword is quite distinct from all the other keywords. Examples of typical keywords are *whop* for the Russian word *klop*, meaning *bedbug*, *top* for the Russian word *tapochkim*, meaning *sandals*, *pot* for the Spanish word *pato* (pronounced, approximately, 'poto'), and *eye* for the Spanish word *caballo* (pronounced 'cob-eye-yo'), meaning *horse*. Students can devise their own keywords if necessary. It is usually more practicable for the instructor to provide students with suitable keywords.

Like some of the organizing activities that were described earlier, the keyword method appears to be somewhat cumbersome: it appears to make vocabulary learning more complicated, rather than easier. Nevertheless, it is effective, because like the organizing strategies we have described it has the effect of changing the learning requirement from the difficult single task of forming a learned link between unrelated words into two much easier tasks.

A number of studies have demonstrated that the technique can be very helpful for students engaged in learning foreign languages. For instance, the college students who participated in one study (Atkinson, 1975) learned forty Russian words on each of three successive days. The learning procedure was one in which a student would hear the Russian word pronounced three times, and simultaneously the English translation of the word would be displayed on a screen. In the keyword condition the keyword would be displayed at the same time. To test learning, the Russian word was pronounced and students were required to type the correct English equivalent.

On each of the three days those students who used the keyword technique learned substantially more words than students who followed an otherwise identical learning procedure without the keywords. After the three-day period students were tested again on all 120 words. At this point, those students who used the keyword method correctly recalled 72 per cent of the items, whereas the other subjects recalled only 46 per cent. In order to assess whether this advantage would be maintained over a substantial period of time, the students were tested again six weeks later. On this occasion the students who had used keywords recalled 43 per cent of the words, and the other students recalled 28 per cent. Thus the keyword method was a highly effective aid to students in this arduous and time-consuming aspect of learning a foreign language.

Further investigations have established the effectiveness of the method for students learning other languages. It has been found that when students can choose whether or not to make use of the method they do use it and they continue to do so on a regular basis over lengthy periods of time, measured in months rather than days. For instance, in one study students who had to learn about 700 Russian words over a nine-week period chose for themselves whether or not to use the method, throughout the entire period. It was found that as time went on they used the method increasingly frequently. Clearly, the effectiveness of the keyword method is not due simply to its novelty.

A keyword method for young children. Does the technique work for young children? Although very young children are quite good at forming images they find it difficult to transfer information from a verbal form into a visual image and back again. Hence, using the keyword method in the manner described above does present some problems to the very young. However, a modified version of the method has been shown to be effective. The modification involves using pictures in addition to the keywords, eliminating the necessity for the learner to produce, unaided, a spontaneous visual image.

Children as young as six years of age can use the modified technique. In one study, six-year-olds recalled eight words out of a list of twelve Spanish words they were taught with the modified keyword method (Pressley, 1977). Children in a control group remembered less than four words, on average.

The keyword method is a flexible device which can be used in a range of situations, not only for acquiring foreign language words. It has also been successfully adapted to helping children to learn word definitions in English (Levin et al., 1982; Sweeney and Bellezza, 1982). Levin and his co-authors used coloured drawings that depicted the concept to be defined, together with a keyword. For example, with the word *pursuade* the chosen keyword was *purse*. There was a picture in which some purses were displayed on a shop stand, and two women were depicted, one of whom said, 'Oh, Martha, you should buy that *purse*,' to which the other replied, 'I think you can *persuade* me to buy it.' Underneath, the word and its definition are written, together with the keyword ('PERSUADE (PURSE) – When you talk someone into doing something'.)

Other mnemonics

There are many other kinds of mnemonics. Some make use of visual imagery, others do not. Recall that the word *mnemonic* is simply a collective term for techniques devised to improve memorization. Common mnemonics that are not based on imagery include rhymes (for instance, 'Thirty days hath September . . .', and 'first-letter' mnemonics, such as 'Richard Of York Gave Battle In Vain', which gives the first letter of each colour in the rainbow in the right order. Both of these types of mnemonics are frequently used by students, and they are usually effective (Gruneberg, 1973).

Mnemonic systems that involve the use of imagery take a number of forms. Examples are the *place method*, in which people visualize familiar locations and then form images connecting those locations with items they wish to remember, and the *peg-word system*, in which learners memorize a short rhyme ('One is a bun, two is a shoe, three is a tree . . .' and so on) and then create images connecting the nouns in the rhyme with the items to be remembered (Howe, 1980).

Methods like these are especially effective for learning lists of items, but imagery-based mnemonics can sometimes be used for learning connected materials. For example, Higbee and Millard (1981) found that a peg-word mnemonic system helped students to learn sayings such as 'One bad apple spoils the barrel' and 'Too many cooks spoil the broth'.

Retrieval

The learners' mental activities that have been described up to this point take place largely or exclusively at the input stage, that is to say at the time when to-be-learned information is initially perceived. In contrast, retrieval activities occur at a much later stage, when an individual needs to locate information that is already retained in memory. As was noted earlier, locating a particular item of information that is stored within a system containing a very large number of items may be a major task. The ease of gaining access to the correct item will depend both upon the manner in which the stored items are arranged and organized and upon the effectiveness of the individual's plans or procedures for locating the required materials.

In the absence of adequate provision for ensuring access to the materials that are retained within a multi-item store, locating whatever is required may be extremely time-consuming. To give a concrete analogy, imagine that there is a library in which a million books are stored but uncatalogued. Assume that a random search is necessary in order to find a particular title, that on average it is necessary to inspect half of the books before the one that we are searching for is found, and that it takes one second to inspect each book. In those circumstances the average time required to locate a particular book would be 500,000 seconds, which is more than five days!

Obviously, the analogy between locating a library book and retrieving items from human memory is far from being a perfect one, but demands upon memory-retrieval mechanisms are of something like this magnitude, at least. The fact that people can gain virtually immediate access to vast quantities of data retained in human memory indicates that highly effective arrangements must exist for enabling people to find stored information when it is required.

On the whole, young children are less successful than older children and adults at locating information stored in memory. They have fewer strategies for locating information, they are less flexible at using and adapting retrieval activities, and they do not possess the older person's ability to invent new retrieval plans in order to deal with the demands of a particular new task. As a result of becoming increasingly good at searching for information and concepts stored in memory the mature individual comes to possess a number of alternative 'routes' for locating required items.

Young children's retrieval skills

Retrieving learned mental skills is in some respects similar to retrieving items of information. When a new skill is first acquired, it tends to be tied to its original context, so far as the young student is concerned. A young child may fail to appreciate the fact that a skill which was acquired in one set of circumstances can also be usefully applied in a variety of different situations. It is as if the only route available to the child for locating that skill is via the particular circumstances present when the skill was first acquired.

Applying the skill more widely, and *transferring* it to new and unfamiliar situations, is only possible if the individual has appropriate ways of retrieving the skill from memory. Otherwise, although the child may possess a certain skill that has the potential of being widely applicable, it may only be actually accessible in a much narrower range of situations. A consequence of becoming a competent learner, and good at knowing how to learn, is that a person acquires considerable expertise in searching for and retrieving the knowledge and skills he has been able to retain. The good learner can quickly find what he knows, and use it. We need to remind ourselves that young children are less able in this respect. They may need guidance in locating their own knowledge and skills. In order to transfer and apply their abilities effectively they also have to acquire other skills, notably those of retrieval.

Although young children often fail to carry out retrieval activities that are necessary for succeeding at school tasks, they can generally learn to do so when given training or guidance. For instance, a study by Kobigasigawa (1974) showed that when six-year-olds were given cues to direct their retrieval activities, their level of success in a word-memory task was equal to that of twelve-year-olds. However, when no cues were provided, and subjects had to rely on their own strategy for locating the items they were retaining, recall decreased dramatically, from twenty words out of twenty-four to only ten items. The older children were better at devising strategies for themselves: their recall decreased much less when they had to do this, to around 16 words.

Retrieval skills as a cause of cross-cultural differences

Differences in retrieval skills probably contribute to the superior performance by literate subjects observed in cross-cultural studies of learning language-based materials (Cole et al., 1971). These authors wanted to find out exactly why literate people consistently outperform non-literate people from rural African communities at a range of learning tasks, even when research studies are carefully designed to rule out some of the more obvious reasons, such as differences in familiarity with the materials and differences in grouping and organizational strategies. The one important difference that did emerge between the groups of subjects lay in the extent to which people made use of effective retrieval strategies. The non-literate rural people were not good at doing this.

In one test, the different items to be remembered were presented in categories: to test remembering the investigators asked the subjects to recall all the items in one category at a time. For example, subjects might be first asked to say all the clothes they remembered from the list of items, and next they would be asked to recall the items from one of the other categories. This procedure was especially effective in raising the performance of the unschooled, non-literate, participants. Giving them the category names at the time of recall was beneficial because, it appeared, they had difficulty in retrieving items from memory without assistance.

Conclusion: Helping Young Learners to Succeed

The research into the effects upon learning of individuals' mental activities shows that, to a large extent, the successful learner is quite simply the learner who does the right things. Since it is not difficult either to discover what good learners do – the nature of the strategies, techniques and procedures that form their learning activities – or to teach less successful learners to do the same things, it is clear that giving students appropriate training in learning how to learn can be enormously beneficial.

Does this mean that, given the right training, a child who is a failure at school will become just as competent as the most success-ful? Up to a point, yes. In certain learning tasks, in which success depends almost entirely upon the appropriateness of people's men-tal activities and strategies, the effect of instructional training can be precisely that.

Teaching new strategies to retarded learners

By way of illustration, consider an experiment in which adolescents who were described as being moderately retarded were systemati-cally taught to follow the procedures that highly intelligent learners spontaneously adopt for a simple memory task. The subjects had to look at a list of letters, presented visually, one at a time, in separate transparent windows on a black display panel. Subjects were able to control the rate at which the items were presented: a new letter appeared whenever the subject pressed a button. Afterwards, one of the items would be shown again, but in a different location. At this point the task for the subject was to point to the particular window in which the item had originally appeared.

At first, the retarded adolescents' scores at this memory task were only half those of a comparison group of college students. Then the adolescents were carefully taught to approach the task by doing exactly the same things as the students. For example, they were told to expose the first three or four items quickly, then pause in order to give themselves time for rehearsing the letters as a group, and then expose the final letters fairly rapidly. In addition to the strategy for exposing and rehearsing the items, they were taught an effective plan for scanning the remembered items at the time of recall.

The researchers (Butterfield, Wambold and Belmont, 1973) had started by describing in detail the spontaneous activities that suc-cessful learners perform when they confront the task. Then they had devised a training programme in which they taught subjects to work through a sequence of steps, which formed an effective strategy for remembering.

The training was highly successful. In a number of separate studies the performance of the retarded adolescents improved dramatically. The number of items they correctly recalled more than doubled, reaching the level normally achieved by college students. This result demonstrates that the initial failure of the retarded subjects was not due to any fundamental deficit in their memory or learning processes. They simply failed to control and co-ordinate the appropriate mental activities in a good strategic plan. When they were taught to do this by careful training, memory performance improved very considerably.

Up to a point, then, we can help unsuccessful children and adults to learn better by getting them to do the things that good learners do. But beyond a point this is not possible. If mental activities were the *only* cause of success at learning it would not be difficult to train everyone to achieve the highest levels of efficiency. In fact, perfection is not quite so readily achieved. One important reason for this is that there is another major direct influence upon learning, one that cannot be so readily modified by training. I refer to the influence of the learner's *existing knowledge*. That cause of learning will be discussed in the following chapter.

4

How Learners Use their Existing Knowledge

An Experiment on Sentence Recall

In several instances described in the previous chapter learning was made easier by transforming a task that appeared to be simple into one that was larger and more cumbersome. Here is another such instance.

Students were asked to listen to a sequence of ten simple statements, like these:

The funny man bought a ring.

The bald man read the newspaper.

Afterwards, the students tried to answer questions designed to assess recall of the statements, for example, 'Which man read the newspaper?' On average they gave only four correct answers out of ten. Other students listened to longer statements, including the following:

The funny man bought a ring that squirted water.

The bald man read the newspaper to look for a hat sale.

After listening to ten sentences these students also tried to answer questions testing recall of the content. Their questions were identical to the ones given to the other students. The students in this second group answered around seven questions out of ten correctly, on average. That is, they recalled almost twice as many items as the other subjects, despite the fact that the statements they had listened to were considerably longer.

How is this explained? The experiment (by Bransford et al., 1981) was designed to cast light on the manner in which people make use of their existing knowledge in order to bring meaning to new information. The longer statements included materials that formed links between the sentence contents and information that was already known to the listeners. As a result, the relationship between the different pieces of information in the sentences is no longer quite so arbitrary. The elements of the sentence are now seen to be connected to each other, because each is related to something within the learner's knowledge that forms a link between them. There is no obvious connection between being bald and reading a newspaper: the sentence 'The bald man read the newspaper' contains two separate ideas. But 'to look for a hat sale' provides an understandable reason for the bald man to read the newspaper.

The extra words direct us to information within our existing knowledge that provides a reason for the bald man to read the newspaper. Once our existing knowledge is introduced in this manner, we understand the ideas in the sentence as being connected to one another.

The improved recall of the longer sentences was definitely due to their incorporating information that enabled the different items of information to be linked to one another. Conceivably, similar improvements could be produced by *any* meaningful extensions to the statements. However, students' recall of a third type of sentence provided in this experiment shows that this is not the case. Examples of these sentences are:

The funny man bought the ring that was on sale.

The bald man read the newspaper while drinking coffee.

These sentences were the same length as the ones that the second group of students heard. They were equally meaningful, and probably more 'interesting' to students than the original short sentences. However, when subjects subsequently tried to answer the questions testing recall, their performance was much poorer than in either of the other conditions: they averaged only two correct items out of ten. The beneficial effect of the second of the three conditions was undoubtedly achieved by the links provided in the second group of sentences between the new information and knowledge that the student participants already possessed.

Learning and Knowing

For every individual, learning and remembering is strongly

influenced by what the person already knows. The effects of a learner's existing knowledge can be sufficiently powerful to override the large difference in performance at memory tasks that is normally observed when young children are compared with adults. In one study some ten-year-olds who were good chess players were allowed ten seconds to look at the pieces on a board forming a chess position (Chi, 1978). Afterwards, they tried to place the chess pieces in the correct places on a blank chessboard. The test was then repeated with adults who knew the rules of chess but were not such good players as the children. All the subjects, children and adults, were also given a separate memory test, based on lists of digits.

The adults were much better than the ten-year-olds at recalling digits. This finding is not at all unexpected: adult subjects usually outperform children on simple tasks of learning and remembering. With the chess pieces, however, the situation was reversed: the children did much better than the adults, the average numbers of pieces correctly recalled by the children and the adults being respectively 9.3 and 5.9.

The reason for the child subjects remembering more items than the adults is simply that the children *knew* more about chess. They could use their knowledge in ways that improved performance. For example, they could see that the relationships between the positions of the different pieces were not arbitrary, and they did not need to remember the position of each piece as a separate and isolated item of information.

The age-related differences in learning and remembering that are found in many tasks are due largely, but not entirely, to older people having more knowledge about the material. In one study of memory for words, thirteen-year-olds were initially more successful than ten-year-olds, who in turn did better than seven-year-olds (Ceci and Howe, 1978). But when the task was carefully adapted to ensure that even the youngest children clearly understood all the words and could understand how they were related to some other words that were provided as 'cues' to guide recall, the age difference completely disappeared. Thus, ensuring that the youngest subjects had all the relevant *knowledge* about the items in the task completely eradicated the age difference.

Learning when differences in knowledge and strategies are absent

Let us pause to consider an implication of the evidence we have looked at. It was suggested that differences in people's knowledge form an important cause of variability in skill at learning and remembering. The research findings show that when the circumstances of a memory task are carefully arranged so that the usual age-related differences in knowledge of the task materials are eliminated, the customary result that older children recall more items than younger children does not occur. Now recall that in chapters 2 and 3 we showed that age-related differences in learning are partly caused by differences in learners' activities: older children are better than younger children at undertaking appropriate mental activities and strategies. If both these assertions are correct, we would expect to find that when younger and older children are compared for performance at a learning task which is carefully designed to ensure that the older children can *neither* make use of strategic mental activities that are unavailable to the younger subjects, *nor* make effective use of their greater knowledge, compared with the younger children, the usual differences between children of different ages will be much reduced.

Does this happen? Consider first an experiment in which the possible value for remembering of using either mental strategies or existing knowledge was minimized by using materials that were unusually simple. The participants saw two briefly illuminated lights, several seconds apart, and they simply had to say whether the second light was brighter or dimmer than the first one. This memory task, which involved retaining information about the brightness of a light, is not one in which there is much opportunity for subjects to introduce either mental strategies or existing knowledge (Belmont, 1978). Is there a reduction in the usual age difference in remembering? In fact, eight-year-old children and mentally retarded adults performed just as well as adult people of normal intelligence.

In another experiment children as young as seven years of age were found to be as successful as adult subjects at a memory task in which they looked at series of pictures and subsequently were given a recognition test. Two pictures were displayed to the subjects at a time. One of the pictures was new, but the other had been displayed previously, and a subject had to say which one that was. This finding gives further evidence that when the task is one in which neither subjects' mental strategies nor their own existing knowledge can make a large contribution, the usual performance differences that favour older people over young children tend to disappear.

That is not to say that there are definitely *no* differences in learning and memory between young and older students when the contributions of mental activities and personal knowledge are eliminated. However, the research findings strongly suggest that these factors are responsible for at least a large share of the age-related improvement that is found in many learning and memory tasks.

Knowing and Understanding

Our existing knowledge is vital for understanding new information and new events. In the absence of appropriate knowledge the simplest sentence would make no sense to us at all. It can be useful to remind ourselves how our comprehension of ordinary events is affected by what we know. Consider the following sentence:

The policeman held up his hand and stopped the car.

What does it mean? Before you tell yourself that the meaning is obvious, stop to think what the sentence *could* mean. The phrase 'held up his hand' could mean that the policemen grasped one of his own hands and simply lifted it up. Alternatively, it could mean that the policemen lifted the hand of a suspect or a prisoner. In the case of 'stopped the car' the phrase could mean that the policeman, being enormously strong, exerted his strength and literally forced a moving car to stop.

But when you first read the sentence it is unlikely that you thought of any of these meanings. Most people who see the sentence take it for granted that the intended meaning is the 'conventional' one. But there is nothing in the sentence to indicate that any of the above meanings is not intended. Why should we rule them out?

The answer lies in our own knowledge (Collins and Quillian, 1972). In order to make sense from 'The policeman held up his hand and stopped the car', we have to introduce our existing knowledge – what we already know about the world. Of course, we are not aware of doing so: it happens automatically. Nevertheless, unless we possess an organized long-term memory store of information that can be drawn upon, the sentence can have no meaning for us. If the reader of the sentence came from a country where policemen were never employed for traffic duty he might well have sufficient knowledge to 'understand' the sentence, but fail to see the most common meaning of 'held up his hand'. For such a reader the phrase would be taken to have one of the alternative meanings.

If the phrase 'held up his hand' had occurred in a context that was different from the one in the above example, we would have interpreted it differently. For instance, in.

> Jack damaged his finger. The doctor held up his hand and examined the injury.

the words have an entirely different meaning. Similarly, the interpretation of 'stopped the car' that we rejected when it was in the sentence about the policeman would be perfectly appropriate if we encountered it in the following sentence:

> The charging elephant stopped the car.

Using contextual cues

In the above examples the *context* in which a phrase occurs directs us to that part of our own knowledge which provides the most likely meaning for a particular phrase. There are alternative ways of achieving this. For instance, with materials that are ambiguous, difficult or unfamiliar, titles or sub-headings can be useful for guiding the learner towards those parts of his knowledge that are related to the new information. Thus, when it is presented without a title, many students have difficulty in making sense of a passage that begins as follows:

> With hocked gems financing him
> our hero bravely defied all scornful laughter
> that tried to prevent his scheme
> your eyes deceive
> he had said
> an egg
> not a table
> correctly typifies this unexplored planet
> > (Dooling and Lachman, 1971, p. 217)

On the other hand, students who are given a title in advance, 'Christopher Columbus Discovering America', do not have any trouble in understanding it. The title makes it clear to the reader where the passage 'belongs' within his structured knowledge. Hence there is improved comprehension and an increase in learning.

Costs of using previous knowledge

People are – and have to be – very good at making use of what they already know in order to comprehend and learn from new experiences. Once information is already retained as part of their knowledge, however, most learners are not so good at remembering when, where or how they gained the knowledge. Usually this does not matter, but on some occasions it can be important for someone to know how certain information was first acquired.

Eyewitness testimony. Imagine that you spend part of today reading a story that is already familiar to you. Tomorrow, you look at another version of the same story and you are asked to identify the particular details that appeared in the version you read today. Students were given such a task in an experimental investigation (Kintsch, 1975). They read passages on topics that were already broadly familiar, such as the biblical story of Joseph and his brothers. A day later their ability to distinguish between the content of the particular passage they had read and their background knowledge of the story was tested. The students found this task extremely difficult, and their performance was poor.

There are some circumstances in which the errors that people make because of their not knowing how certain knowledge was acquired can have unfortunate practical consequences. Think about what happens when someone witnesses an accident or a crime, and afterwards is repeatedly asked to describe what was seen. Understandably, mistakes sometimes occur in the descriptions. The problem is that when a person is asked to describe an event for, say, the fifth time, it may be quite impossible for that person to distinguish between his memory for the original event and his memory for his previous recollection of the event. He may *think* he is recalling the actual event, but in fact be retrieving from memory a stored representation that was formed partly by the event itself and partly by subsequent reports in the form of his own attempts to recall it.

The effects are quite innocuous if the earlier attempts at recall are accurate, but if they are inaccurate the individuals's memory for events may become progressively more flawed, without the person being aware of it.

Evidence that errors of this kind can occur is provided by some research studies conducted by Elizabeth Loftus and her colleagues (e.g. Loftus and Palmer, 1974). These researchers were particularly interested in discovering whether people's memory for happenings such as traffic accidents can be influenced by information that is supplied *after* the event. Some people were shown a film of a traffic accident in which two cars collide. Afterwards they were asked to say how fast the vehicles had been moving. However, new information was surreptitiously introduced at this stage by varying the form of the question. Some participants were asked how fast the cars were going when they *hit* each other: others were asked to say how fast the cars were going when they *smashed into* each other.

The participants' estimates of the cars' speed were influenced by the form of the questions asked. Those people who were asked about the speed of cars which smashed into each other reported a higher speed, on average, than those who were told to report the speed of the cars which hit each other. The information that was introduced into the questions had further effects upon the participants' memory for (as they believed) the original accident. For instance, when the people who had seen the film of the accident were asked whether they saw any broken glass, those individuals who had previously been asked the question which included the word 'smashed' were more likely than the others to respond 'Yes'. (In fact, there was no broken glass in the film.) These research findings point to some of the dangers of allowing 'leading questions' either in court or in any procedure that aims to elicit the truth about events which have been witnessed.

Distortions caused by previous knowledge. Another situation in which existing knowledge can sometimes make it more difficult rather than easier to learn new facts occurs when we have to learn something which seems to contradict what we already know. In one study (Ceci, Caves and Howe, 1981) seven-year-olds and ten-year-olds listened to a story in which a variety of well-known characters from television and movies behaved in ways which clashed with the children's knowledge of them. For instance, in the story, the 'Six

Million Dollar Man' was supposed to carry a can of paint, but he could not do so because he was too weak. Children who listened to the story and were tested for recall immediately afterwards had no difficulty in remembering it accurately, however discordant were the actions of the familiar characters with the children's knowledge of them. But if the recall test was delayed by several weeks, recall of the events in the story was not only less accurate but systematically distorted in the direction of the children's prior knowledge of the people in the story.

It seems that when retention of information and events is less than perfect, people make *inferences* about them, based on prior knowledge, often without knowing that they are doing so. At school, students sometimes need to acquire new knowledge that appears to contradict what they already know. Both teachers and students need to be aware of the distorting influences that existing knowledge can have in these circumstances.

On some occasions existing knowledge can make it harder rather than easier to remember facts about other people, particularly when our personal beliefs, opinions or prejudices are involved. Our existing views about others can impede learning. Sometimes, beliefs and prejudices can distort *perception* of what actually happens, but even when perception is accurate existing knowledge in the form of ideas and opinions that are central to our beliefs can form further obstacles to learning. This is illustrated by a study in which university students read a 750-word passage that described the life of a woman named Betty (Snyder and Uranowitz, 1978). The students read about various aspects of Betty's life, including her childhood, home life, relationships with her parents, and a number of other matters. One week after the students had read the passage they were given a 36-item multiple-choice test in order to assess how well they had retained the biographical information about Betty. Some of the test questions asked about Betty's relationships with people of both sexes. For instance, one multiple-choice question asked whether Betty occasionally dated men, never went out with men, or went steady. The first choice, that she occasionally dated men, was the correct one.

The students' responses to the questions showed that their memory for facts about Betty's life could be strongly influenced by information that was supplied *after* they had read the passage, if it made contact with their beliefs about people. In the experiment, after the students had finished reading about Betty, some of them were told that she now lives as a lesbian; others were informed that her life-style is that of a heterosexual person. Despite the fact that, prior to this, all the students had received exactly the same information about the various facts of Betty's life, those participants who were subsequently told that Betty was a lesbian were more likely than the others to recall (incorrectly) that she never went out with men. Conversely, students who were told that that she was heterosexual often recalled (equally wrongly) that Betty 'went steady'.

In the process of education students quite often need to learn ideas and facts that contradict their established views and preconceptions. Knowing that a learner's prior 'knowledge' (the inverted commas being added to extend the word's meaning to all that a learner *believes* to be true), which normally aids learning and makes it easier for a student to retain new information, can also have a very different effect should alert the teacher to the problems that can sometimes arise.

Advance Organizers for Classroom Learning

Every good teacher knows that students acquire new knowledge most easily when the new information bears some relationship to existing knowledge, and is not totally unfamiliar. Information will not be meaningful to a person unless he can relate it to what is already familiar. In everyday life we are constantly using *metaphors*. Metaphors provide a way of expressing new meanings in terms of highly familiar concepts, such as buildings (for example, 'Is that the *foundation* for your theory? We need to *buttress* the theory with *solid* arguments'), food ('All this article has in it are *raw facts*, *half-baked ideas*, and *warmed-over theories*'), plants ('That's a *budding* theory. The other idea *died on the vine*') or even people ('This theory *gave birth* to many ideas, but those ideas *died off* in the Middle Ages') (Lakoff and Johnson, 1980).

In school learning, as D. P. Ausubel (1968) has emphasized, however logical and sensible is the material that students are required to learn, if it is not understandable to a particular individual, that person cannot acquire it in a meaningful fashion.

It is quite possible for learning to be non-meaningful even when the learned information is inherently meaningful. This is demonstrated by an experience described in an account of a school visit by the educational philosopher John Dewey (Bloom, 1956, p. 29). Dewey, who was observing teaching in a classroom, asked the pupils a question, 'What would happen if you were to dig an immensely deep hole into the earth?' The students responded with silence and blank stares. After a pause the teacher muttered something about the question being wrong, and turning to the children he asked, 'What is the state of the centre of the earth?' This time the children all answered immediately with the correct answer, 'Igneous fusion'. It is clear that although the children had learned 'the answer' they had really acquired little more than a sequence of words (the answer) to be uttered as a response to another sequence of words (the question). This is hardly a satisfactory state of affairs.

To ensure that a particular item of knowledge can be meaningfully learned it may be necessary for the teacher to help the student by showing how whatever is to be acquired can be connected to something that the learner already knows. Alternatively, if that is not possible, a similar result may be achieved by first supplying the learner with knowledge that can perform a 'bridging' function, by connecting the new information to existing knowledge. Ausubel has suggested that teachers should devise *advance organizers* to perform the bridging operation. Essentially, an advance organizer is a piece of information that readily connects to a person's existing knowledge, and is also conceptually linked to the new material to be learned. After being exposed to the advance organizer the learner is in a position to acquire the new, now meaningful, information.

Intuitively, the idea of providing advance organizers makes good sense. Indeed, it is widely accepted that in order to teach people about a particular topic it is wise to find out what they already know in relation to the topic, and take that existing knowledge as the 'point of departure' for commencing instruction. The precise forms of advance organizers can vary according to particular circumstances. For situations where the new material is entirely unfamiliar to the learner, Ausubel recommends devising an organizer which is largely 'expository'.

For example, a suitable organizer to precede the teaching of Darwin's theory to a totally naive student might be a prose passage showing how Darwin's ideas are related to the learner's general knowledge, and providing a framework summarizing the major ideas in the theory, to form 'anchoring' concepts for the details of the theory. In other circumstances a different kind of organizer might be more appropriate. For example, for a student who needs to gain detailed knowledge of one technique of life saving and has already learned about a different method, the most effective kind of organizer might be one which directs the learner's attention to some of the similarities and the differences between the two methods. Such an organizer would not in itself provide much new information, but it would help the learner to make optimum use of existing knowledge.

Research studies designed to evaluate advance organizers have shown that they can be helpful in a range of situations. However, organizers are not easy to devise, and they provide no instant cure for learning problems. A major practical difficulty resides in the fact that in order to design a maximally effective advance organizer for teaching particular materials to a particular individual, it is necessary to ascertain fairly precisely the present state of the individual's knowledge in relation to the topic. Doing so may not be at all easy.

The idea of using advance organizers is both appealing and sensible, although the practical difficulties involved in devising materials that successfully fulfil that function may be considerable. Furthermore, progressing from a state of ignorance about an area of knowledge to one of expertise and knowledgeability may involve considerably more than simply acquiring a greater amount of information. Very often, learning also involves gaining a deeper understanding of something, or a new perspective on the knowledge content.

Learning Unfamiliar Topics

Some of the research by John Bransford and his colleagues (Bransford et al., 1981) provides some interesting further insights into the ways in which existing knowledge influences learning and also into the manner in which learning contributes to the growth of a person's knowledge. They ask, for example, how a novice at biology might learn about the nature and functions of veins and arteries. What would such a person learn from the statement that arteries, which are thick and elastic, carry from the heart blood that is rich in oxygen, while veins, which are thinner than arteries and more elastic, carry blood that is rich in carbon dioxide back to the heart?

These authors point out that what a person will actually learn from reading this statement will depend very considerably upon that individual's previous knowledge. For a student who knows nothing at all of biology and is ignorant of the workings of the heart, the above description would be essentially little more than a series of isolated and separate facts. It would be very difficult to learn. In order to perceive the statement as being a meaningful one, in which the different facts and ideas are connected to each other, the learner must already possess considerable knowledge about the items and concepts mentioned in the statement, and their implications. The statement is meaningful, connected and easy to learn if, and only if, the learner already knows enough about its contents to be able to provide connections between its parts and and to introduce sufficient familiar facts and images to make its meanings apparent. Only if the learner can introduce various kinds of pertinent information from his own knowledge base will the connectedness between the different parts of the statement be clear.

Making the unfamiliar more familiar

Bransford and his co-authors make a number of suggestions about things that a student might do to make the information in the above statement about the heart less arbitrary and more familiar. For example, making an image of an artery in the form of a thick hollow tube might help a student to remember the fact that arteries are thick. A visual image in which the tube is seen to be suspended by a stretching and contracting elastic band, which causes the tube to move, might help the student to remember that arteries are elastic. The image might be further embellished, they suggest, by including a Valentine's Day depiction of a heart, from which blood is pouring towards the tube, perhaps accompanied by bubbles that are round in shape, like a series of Os, representing oxygen.

Forming a composite visual image would be one way – not the only way or necessarily the best way – in which a student might make the information in the statement more understandable and familiar, and form connections between the different parts. The individual uses existing knowledge as a basis for ideas and images that give meaning and connectedness to the passage as a whole. A student whose knowledge of biology is more advanced would act differently: he might well consider the above image-making activities not only inappropriate but actually misleading.

Such images *are* misleading, beyond a certain point. On the one hand they would be helpful for a beginner who lacks the concepts necessary for immediately understanding the actions of veins and arteries. But for a more advanced student, who required an accurate understanding of the concepts, the kinds of images that have been suggested could be counterproductive because the manner in which they depict the biological processes is oversimplified and distorting.

It is quite often the case that the images, metaphors and analogies which teachers introduce in order to make the unfamiliar more familiar, and to direct learners to relationships or similarities between new material and what is already known, do introduce such distortions. Consequently, understanding and learning of the new concepts is incomplete and inaccurate. Often this is inevitable. If there is a large gap between what is to be learned and what is already known the best that can be hoped for is a partial closing of the gap, or some advance *towards* full understanding.

Learning How to Make Use of Previous Knowledge

The successful learner, when confronted by information that seems to be unfamiliar, is good at searching through his own knowledge base in order to find facts or concepts that can be used to reduce the unfamiliarity of the new data. Making use of effective retrieval skills (chapter 3), he looks for existing knowledge that can be introduced to clarify new facts or form links between them. In a sense, such a learner is doing much of the work of constructing an advance organizer.

The experiments by Bransford and his co-authors that were described at the beginning of the chapter were designed to verify the fact that learning can be increased by directing people towards those parts of their prior knowledge that can clarify the relationship between new facts that are apparently arbitrary. Some further studies were designed to investigate how learners actively make use of their knowledge in order to learn new materials. One experiment demonstrated that the extent to which learning the information in sentences like the ones used in the experiments described previously is improved by students' drawing upon their own existing knowledge partly depends upon the particular kinds of questions that the learners ask themselves.

College students were shown sentences such as 'The tall man bought the crackers'. They were asked to make up a phrase that completed each statement, by responding either to the question 'What might happen next?' or to the question 'Why might each type of man perform a particular act?' The students who received the second type of question not only generated phrases that were judged to clarify the significance of the original sentence information more precisely, but also recalled the contents more accurately. You may recall a similar finding in the previous chapter. To demonstrate the importance of learners' *activities*, an experiment was described in which children who were told to answer questions about the relationship between two pictured objects (Turnure, Buium and Thurlow, 1976) recalled more items than children who were given alternative study instructions. At that point, emphasis was placed upon the importance of learners' activities. Alternatively, we might have noted that the question-asking activity was effective because it provided a way of locating some data from the children's *knowledge* that provided a connection between otherwise arbitrary objects.

Further research by Bransford has established that by 11 years of age some children are good at judging that stories made from non-arbitrary sentences (e.g. 'The hungry boy had eaten a hamburger') are easier to learn than stories containing arbitrary sentences (e.g. 'The hungry boy had taken a nap'). Such children can guide their study efforts in accordance with their judgements of task difficulty, spending more time studying the stories they judge to be harder to learn.

Another study investigated how 11-year-olds activated their own knowledge in order to clarify information they were learning. A number of sentences were presented, for example 'The hungry man got into the car'. The students were told to add to each sentence a phrase that would help them to remember it. They were divided into three groups, academically less successful, average and successful, as assessed by teacher ratings and test scores. It was found that those children who were rated as being successful at school produced more precise clarifying phrases than the other students. They also recalled more items correctly when given questions such as 'Which man got into the car?'; they recalled most accurately those sentences for which they had added the most precise clarifying phrases, and they were better than the other children at explaining the reasons why precise clarifying phrases led to increased recall.

In short, the students who were successful at school were better than the others at making use of their own knowledge when confronted by a learning task containing new and unrelated facts, and the successful students were also more aware of their reasons for introducing information from their own existing knowledge.

Training studies

Gaining the ability to make effective use of one's own knowledge is an important aspect of learning how to learn. Bransford and his colleagues have been interested in devising ways to teach children how to activate those parts of their knowledge that can be effective in clarifying the significance of new information. They found that simply explaining how relevant elaborations such as 'The hungry man got into the car and drove to the restaurant' can facilitate learning only helped to a limited extent. It was not enough to give training that just consisted of demonstrating to the students the value of using phrases to provide the kind of clarification that is absent when sentences are simply extended (e.g. 'The hungry man got into the car and drove to work').

There was much more success with training that was carefully designed to ensure that children really understood why certain kinds of extensions to sentences made them clearer. The children were first encouraged to discover for themselves the difficulty of learning arbitrarily related facts. They listened to some arbitrary sentences and were later questioned about them. The poor level of performance at this stage demonstrated to the children that the sentences were difficult to learn. Then the children were encouraged to ask themselves questions about the sentences. It was intended that this should help them see that the sentences were indeed arbitrary. For example, with 'The kind man bought the milk' a child might be asked 'Is there any more reason to mention that a kind man bought milk than a tall man, a mean man?'

The next step in the training involved prompting the children to activate information from their own knowledge that would make the sentence relationships (for example, between the 'kindness' and the 'milk-buying' in 'The kind man bought the milk') seem less arbitrary. For instance, a child might be asked, 'Why might a kind man be buying milk?' When the child provided reasons which could be used to form extensions to a sentence, he was encouraged to ask further questions aimed at evaluating the sentence extensions he had suggested. For example, if a child had suggested 'Because he was thirsty', he might be asked 'What does this have to do with being kind? Wouldn't a mean man be just as likely to do the same thing?' (Bransford et al., 1981, p. 103). After they had received training in which they were asked questions like this, and encouraged to generate similar questions for themselves, all the 11-year-olds gained the ability to produce sentence extensions that successfully performed the function of clarifying the initial short sentence by relating the different parts of it to each other, as in 'The kind man bought the milk *to give to the hungry child*'.

Assessing the results of training. To test the effectiveness of the training, the children were given the memory test they had started with, and on which they had originally performed very poorly. This time, instead of correctly answering only one or two questions out of ten, most of the children did perfectly. They also found the task exciting and enjoyable. When they were asked to provide sentences which would transform short arbitrary sentences into ones that were meaningful and non-arbitrary, over 90 per cent of the elaborations they gave were ones that achieved this function effectively.

These findings demonstrate that it is undoubtedly possible to teach children successful strategies for activating their own knowledge in ways that make new information easier to learn. Some children need considerable prompting and help: it would be unwise to assume that all students find it easy to learn such strategic skills. As with the learned strategies described in the previous chapter, many children need considerable practice before they can gain the habit of regularly making use of their existing knowledge in the most effective ways. Also, the usual problems of limited transfer arise. Spontaneous generalizing and application of the newly acquired strategies to different kinds of circumstances are unlikely to occur until the strategies become firmly established.

Nevertheless, the ability to introduce one's own knowledge with maximum effectiveness when learning new information is potentially so extremely valuable and widely applicable that time and effort spent in helping children to learn the necessary skills is indeed well spent. Quite apart from the obvious improvements in learning it produces, this ability makes the activity of reading considerably more interesting to a child. Bransford and his co-authors point out that as a way to learn material from prose passages, merely rereading the information is not only inefficient but also boring. The individual who regularly brings what he already knows to his own learning activities finds the experience much more fruitful and interesting. Concerning good learners, they write:

> They seem able to place themselves in the role of an explorer or detective who searches for the significance of facts. Learners who fail to do this, who merely reread the sentences in a passage, for example, may find the experience uninteresting and tedious. The processes that underlie effective learning may therefore be related to those that capture students' interest, that motivate them to learn.' (Bransford et al., 1981, pp. 107–8)

The Representation of Knowledge

It can be extremely valuable for the teacher to know what a student already knows. Existing knowledge provides the starting-point for new school learning. A teacher who was armed with a precise and detailed specification of a particular student's knowledge – all the facts, concepts, ideas and skills stored within that person's cognitive structures – would be ideally equipped to maximize learning.

Psychologists have been aware of the potential practical value of exhaustively describing the knowledge that learners already possess. They have been especially interested in trying to find out how knowledge is actually represented within the mental structures that control human cognition. Discovering how knowledge is represented in a person's brain may appear to be an easy task: in fact it is not. The most elementary questions are difficult to answer. How is the knowledge arranged? How many levels of organization are involved? Is the information stored in the brain language-based? (The fact that information is *received* by the human learner in language form does not guarantee that the same language plays an identical part in the brain's *retention* of the information, just as, with a computer, the fact that input may be language-based does not mean that the computer's internal operations involve information in the same language form.) Does the brain retain images that are not language-based? Cognitive psychologists are fascinated by questions like these, but final answers are proving hard to obtain.

For educators, progress towards a better understanding of the mental structures that underlie knowledge and cognition will ultimately bring great practical benefits. At this point, it will suffice to mention a few of the ideas that have guided research into this topic.

Representation of dinosaur knowledge in a young child

One approach is to begin by investigating bodies of knowledge that are relatively small and limited in scope. In practice, appropriate instances are not easy to locate, since in most people knowledge about one topic is closely linked to knowledge of other things. However, the authors of one study (Chi and Koeske, 1983) were able to avoid a number of problems by studying a young boy, aged four, who happened to possess a sizeable body of knowledge about dinosaurs. The boy's knowledge about dinosaurs, whilst remarkable for a child of his age, was sufficiently limited for it to be possible for the experimenter to ascertain fairly precisely what he did know about dinosaurs. Also, the investigation was made easier by the fact that what the boy knew about dinosaurs was relatively separate from and independent of his knowledge in other areas.

The authors were particularly interested in how the boy's knowledge was *structured*. The effect of learning is not simply to increase the size of a person's knowledge. Equally importantly, there are organizational changes, reflecting the way information is structured. Changes in the structure of what a person knows have implications for future learning.

To study the implications of differences in the structuring of knowledge, Chi and Koeske examined two sub-sets of knowledge within the same boy. They did this by forming one list of dinosaurs which he was well informed about, and a second list of dinosaurs for which his knowledge was much sparser. As they had expected, the boy performed better on learning and memory tasks involving the sub-set of dinosaurs about which he was more knowledgeable.

A major aim of Chi and Koeske's study was to gain a better

understanding of *why* this was so. They were interested in discovering the precise reasons for people being more successful at those learning tasks in which the materials are highly familiar. In this case they considered two contributing factors: first, knowing more in the simple sense of knowing about a greater number of properties of an item, and, second, the way information is organized within the structured knowledge base of an individual. They found that the simple amount of the boy's knowledge, that is the number of an item's properties that were familiar to him, did not have a very strong influence on his performance. Organizational and structural factors, on the other hand, had much more powerful effects.

The boy's recall and retention of lists of dinosaurs was found to be strongly influenced by the extent to which the composition of the lists matched the organized structure of his knowledge. Important factors were the number of links, in the boy's knowledge base, between the different items in list of dinosaurs, and the strength of the linkages, and the patterning of the links between the items.

There is a clear practical implication of this finding. It is that, in order to maximize effective classroom learning, we should have a full understanding of how a student's knowledge is organized and interrelated: just knowing what the learner knows about individual facts and concepts is not enough.

Hierarchical representation of items' properties

A second approach that aims to shed light on the manner in which knowledge is represented starts by suggesting a straightforward way in which related facts and concepts *could* conceivably be represented. If a person's knowledge is actually organized in that way, we should be able to make certain predictions. For example, tasks in which we need to bring together items of information that are adjacent within the structure of a person's knowledge should be performed more easily or more accurately than tasks involving the bringing together of more distant items. If the predictions that we make on the assumption that our guesses about the way in which knowledge is represented in a learner's memory structure prove to be accurate, this would indicate that our hypothesized structure corresponds with the actual organization that exists. Conversely, wrong predictions would indicate that the suggested representation of knowledge does not correspond with reality.

Such an approach was followed by Collins and Quillian (1969). They suggested that some kinds of information about objects and their properties might be represented hierarchically, on a number of separate levels. Level One, the top level, represents a very broad class of objects, 'animals', and lists attributes of animals in general. On the lower levels there are successively smaller classes of items, together with their attributes, the classes at each of the levels being sub-categories of those at the level above.

Collins and Quillian asked some students to perform a number of tasks that were designed to show whether or not such a representation bears any resemblance to the way in which information about these items and their attributes is actually represented in the organization of a person's body of knowledge. If their suggestion about hierarchical representation of objects and their properties really does correspond with how a person's knowledge is really structured, it ought to follow that tasks which involve a person bringing together items of information that are depicted as being widely separated will take longer to perform than tasks that involve items of information that are adjacent to each other. For example, the question 'Is a canary yellow?' can be answered from information that is all stored at one mode, according to Collins and Quillian. However, to answer 'Does a canary have gills?' it would be necessary (if knowledge is structured in the hierarchical manner they suggest) to transmit information between nodes that are widely separated, in order to bring together all the information that is needed to answer the question. Hence it is possible to get some idea of how accurately their hierarchical model depicts how knowledge is actually represented in human memory by seeing whether the relative times that students take to respond to various questions corresponds with predictions generated by the hierarchical model. Students were asked to decide on the truth or falsity of various propositions, and the time taken to respond was recorded. The propositions included the following:

An ostrich can move around
A canary has gills
Salmon is edible
A shark has wings
A fish can swim

Making predictions and testing them. If the hierarchical model of Collins and Quillian does provide an accurate representation of the organization of a person's knowledge, the time that is taken to decide about the truth of, say, 'Salmon is edible' will be shorter than the time necessary for deciding that, for instance, 'A shark has wings'. In order to decide about the latter proposition it is necessary to retrieve and combine information from separate points that are at different levels. With the first statement this is not necessary. The authors predicted that the response time for verifying a statement would be directly related to the number of levels between which information would need to be transferred.

Their findings were broadly in line with the predictions. Thus the average time to respond to a question based on information that is all represented at the same level (for example, 'A canary can sing') was shorter than the time to respond to a question requiring information stored at adjacent levels (for example, 'A canary can fly'). This in turn was shorter than the time needed for questions using information from non-adjacent levels (for example, 'A canary has skin'). These results provide a degree of support for the view that the manner in which objects and their attributes were depicted by Collins and Quillian, involving hierarchical organization into broad classes and narrower sub-categories, does bear a resemblance to the manner in which information is actually represented in the knowledge stores of real people.

This research is undoubtedly ingenious, and it provides an interesting way of trying to make progress towards the highly desirable goal of discovering how knowledge is represented within human cognitive structures. However, various findings from more recent work have not been in accord with the predictions about relative response times that are generated by depictions in which knowledge organization is seen as being hierarchical, involving a number of separate but linked levels. For example, a multi-level hierarchical representation would generate the prediction that when questions are asked about items of information that are said to be stored at the same level within a semantic hierarchy (for example, 'Is a cantaloupe a melon?') they would be answered more quickly than questions involving information at different levels (for example, 'Is a cantaloupe a fruit?'). In fact, experimental research has established that that is by no means always the case (Rips, Shoben and Smith, 1973). Also, a study by Carol Conrad (1972) showed that varying the form of the assertions that subjects were required to verify led to differences in the pattern of response times that would not have been expected if the structures as depicted by Collins and Quillian accurately represent reality. They asked people to decide on the truth of lists of statements in which the sentence subject was retained but the predicate varied, as in:

A canary has skin

A canary can fly

Conrad, on the other hand, presented sequences of sentences in which the subject varied, as in:

An animal has skin

A bird has skin

This ought to make no difference to the response times, but it does, a fact which provides evidence of deficiencies in the organizational structures suggested by Collins and Quillian. Almost certainly, the manner in which they depict the representation of knowledge in the human mind is too simple to be accurate. In reality, the way in which people's knowledge is structured is more complex, and, to make matters even more complicated, reflects factors that are unique to each individual. Nevertheless, that which a person knows must be arranged, patterned and organized in *some* describable manner, and in principle it ought to be possible for psychologists to be able to describe how. The approach of Collins and Quillian can be seen as an imaginative attempt to move in that direction. For teachers, the practical value of being able to make accurate descriptions of how a particular child's knowledge is actually represented will be enormous.

Scripts and schemas

The third and final approach that we shall consider gives attention to the representation of themes and sequences of events. Words such as *schema* and *script* frequently occur in descriptions of this research, which has been influenced by some early investigations of people's memory for stories, undertaken in the 1920s by F. C. Bartlett. He defined a schema as 'an active organization of past reactions, or of past experiences, which must always be supposed to be operating in any well-adapted response' (Bartlett, 1932, p. 201).

Bartlett, who was one of the first psychologists to develop the view that knowledge was represented in the form of unconscious mental structures, considered that the different schemas operate not separately but as a unitary mass. Most importantly, he considered that following exposure to many events and items of information the brain retains some kind of 'generic cognitive representation', or schema, containing the essential structures or elements that a large number of informational inputs have in common. Some modern psychologists prefer to use the word *script*, but with essentially the same meaning. Thus,

> As an economy measure in the storage of episodes, when enough of them are alike they are remembered in terms of a standardized, generalized episode which we will call a script. (Schank and Abelson, 1977, p. 19)

When an individual is exposed to information that is new and unfamiliar he is said to make an 'effort after meaning', by attempting to relate the new material to the contents of an existing schema. So far as learning is concerned, doing so is very useful, since there is much evidence that information related to a schema or script (or 'theme') is better remembered than information that is not related to any schema of the learner.

In recent years considerable emphasis has been given to the importance of schemas or scripts for learning and understanding. They provide frames of reference that help us to comprehend and remember events we experience, by serving as frameworks of organized knowledge to which new events can be connected. Look at this little story:

> John went to a restaurant. He asked the waitress for *coq au vin*. He paid the check and left.

Although it is short, it seems quite meaningful. The reader has a fair idea of what happened. But notice how much it does *not* say. For instance, there is no mention of whether John found a free table in the restaurant, or if he sat down to eat. The account does not even specify that John ate from a plate, or used a knife and fork.

Nevertheless, we, the readers, assume that these events probably did occur. Why? Because we *infer* them on the basis of our stored knowledge about the kinds of things that normally happen when a person goes for a meal in a restaurant. Within our knowledge there is something that we might call a 'going-for-a-meal-in-a-restaurant script', representing the bare bones of such events, the essential structure that is common to most actual visits by individuals to particular restaurants. A person who has been to restaurants on a number of occasions will have acquired a schema (or script) that contains information about the likely sequence of events: we know what it is like to have a meal in a restaurant. Because we possess an appropriate schema, we can fill the gaps in the account of John's visit to the restaurant. It is a meaningful account, but only by virtue of the fact that we already have the necessary schema, or script.

Knowledge in the form of scripts also enables people to understand instructions and follow procedures that would otherwise be incomprehensible. Consequently, we can catch trains from unfamiliar stations or visit a theatre for the first time without having to learn the appropriate procedures from scratch. In each of these situations we know, at least in a general way, how things are done (Schank and Abelson, 1977).

For school learning, it is especially important to realize that schema-related information is relatively easy to comprehend and learn. The young child who lacks appropriate schemas will find a story or an account of events hard to remember. In children, possession of a schema does not guarantee that it will be used effectively for aiding learning, but it has been shown that seven-year-olds who do not initially use such knowledge can quite easily be trained to do so (Buss et al., 1983). They found that older children and college students used their knowledge of conventional forms of story structures to aid retention of stories that were presented in a 'scrambled' form. The younger children could also do so, after a brief training procedure.

Even the most ordinary actions are better remembered when they form part of a schema-related sequence. A study by Brewer and Dupree (1983) showed that simple activities such as walking into a room, removing clothes, picking up objects and moving them around, and looking at a watch, were much more often recalled when they formed part of a 'plan schema' (for example, opening a drawer in order to take out a stapler) than when they did not (for example, simply opening a drawer). The implication for school learning is that the likelihood of a student retaining some information about events and activities can be usefully increased by placing the information within the context for which an existing schema is already available.

5

The Child who Arrives at School

The child who arrives at school for the first time is by no means new to the business of learning. This young person will have already notched up some massive learned achievements, and will have become a highly experienced learner in some respects. But although all five- and six-year-olds are capable learners, children do vary considerably in the extent to which their lives before school have prepared them for the particular kinds of learning that are crucial in school education.

In this chapter and the next we shall look at some of the characteristics of children, in particular those attributes that are important for success at school. Some of the special demands of school learning will be discussed. We shall remove some confusion surrounding the question of whether certain achievements in children are most accurately regarded as being caused by learning or by human development. We shall introduce concepts such as 'ability' and 'intelligence' and look at some evidence concerning hereditary influences. The possible implications for learning of 'critical periods' will be examined.

Learning In and Out of School

School learning is different in many ways from the learning that takes place out of school. For most children there are major differences between school and home in the kinds of things that are learned and the forms of learning that are emphasized. There are also important differences in the circumstances in which learning occurs.

School makes many demands upon the young learner that are different from those typically experienced in everyday life at home. Language is undoubtedly important at home as a medium of communication, but at school language alone has to carry burdens which at home are shared between language and other aids to learning. For example, the teacher may have to rely exclusively on language to give information or communicate instructions to a fairly large number of children. The beginning student may be more familiar with one-to-one learning situations, in which the mother who teaches her child can supplement language with non-verbal communication, often using facial expressions. She can also demonstrate things to her child or intervene in various ways if she thinks her child needs assistance (Wachs and Gruen, 1982).

School gives prominence to the acquisition of intellectual skills and knowledge rather than movement-based abilities, to abstract and symbolic achievements rather than concrete ones, and to abilities that are necessary for long-term achievements rather than ones which have immediate practical value for the learner. Learning in school is very often deliberate, involving a definite intention to learn or remember. At home, on the other hand, it is unusual for a child to engage in an activity with the express purpose of learning or remembering something. Despite all that he has learned, the pre-school child may not be at all familiar with the meaning of sentences like 'Try to learn this', or 'I want you to remember. . .'.

As was demonstrated in chapter 2, learning frequently takes place in the absence of any deliberate intent or effort to learn, simply as a result of the mental processing that takes place when a person perceives and experiences events in everyday life. For many children, it is only when school begins that it becomes necessary to set out to learn information or acquire skills that are not closely bound to ongoing activities, or to confront a task in which learning is the explicit goal. Furthermore, for most children, the kinds of learning tasks that make it necessary for the individual to have definite plans or strategies for learning or remembering are first encountered at school.

Even without considering the vital school-taught skills of literacy and numeracy, it is easy to see that despite all the child's experience as a learner, some unfamiliar and difficult challenges must be faced when school begins. We have already noted that children differ very considerably in the extent to which pre-school experiences have prepared them for school learning. But even for the best-prepared, learning at school is not simply a continuation of home life. Its demands are new and difficult.

Contrasting tasks of home and school

An experiment conducted in the USSR provides a fascinating illustration of the contrasting ways in which young children cope with learning tasks that are typical of ones experienced at home and ones that are encountered for the first time when a child goes to school. In the study, some young children simply listened to lists of five words for common objects such as *carrot, milk* and *socks*. They were told to try to remember as many items as they could. Sixty seconds later they were asked to say all the words they could recall.

Predictably, older children did better at this task than the youngest subjects. The oldest, aged between six and seven years, remembered on average 2.3 words out of 5, but the average recall of the youngest subjects, who were aged three and four years, was only 0.6 words. Clearly, none of the children did very well at this task, but the youngest subjects performed particularly badly.

Why did they do so poorly? Perhaps the children were simply not capable of remembering the information. However, another possibility is that the answer lies in the kind of memory task that was used. It is hardly the sort of task that would be particularly familiar to children before they go to school, nor is it one that would seem to be very interesting or meaningful to pre-school children. For children who have spent some time at school, however, such a task would seem less unfamiliar.

Some other young children were given a task that was less strange to them than the one described above, but which required them to remember exactly the same information. These children were busily engaged in a game of shopping. At one point in the game each child listened to the same list of words that the other children heard, but the task for the second group of children was different: they had to go to the 'shop' (at the other end of the room) and ask for the items on the list. These children did very much better than the others. The number of words they recalled averaged 3.8 for the six- to seven-year-olds, and 1.0 for the three- to four-year-olds.

Note that the formal requirements of the memory tasks were the same for the two groups of children. All the children heard the same words, then they had to retain them for the same amount of time, and subsequently they tried to recall the words. The difference between the two groups of children lay in the familiarity of the situation and what it meant to them. Those children who were playing at shopping had a reason, which they could understand, for remembering the items. These children, unlike the others, performed the memory task in the context of activities with a goal that was highly meaningful to them. There was nothing strange or artificial about the task.

The findings of this experiment demonstrate that young children are by no means incapable of remembering, but that they do poorly in unfamiliar situations in which remembering something is itself the main goal, rather than a way of achieving some meaningful end result. In school, activities in which the main purpose is to learn or remember something are fairly common: children who have been at school for several years will have learned to cope with situations in which they are instructed to learn some new knowledge or information. But when they first go to school, many children will not have experienced such tasks. They will have to start learning how to deal with these unfamiliar demands.

The school's demands

Adults react in different ways to evidence of the discontinuities between the circumstances of school learning and those in which the child learns in day-to-day life at home. A possible response is to say that such discontinuities simply demonstrate the artificiality or 'unnaturalness' of school, and to demand that educators should strive to make the experience of school much closer to that of 'real life'. People who are in sympathy with this view would urge teachers to eliminate the separation between learning, living and doing. It is sometimes claimed that schools seem to encourage such a separation.

I shall not go into the arguments for and against this kind of view. Undoubtedly, psychological evidence does support the suggestion that new learning must be relatable to a child's existing knowledge and skills, as was shown in chapter 4. However, to criticize school learning because it is 'artificial' in the sense of not being immediately relevant to the child's here-and-now experience of daily living, or to castigate schools as being 'unnatural' for this reason is to miss much of the point of school education.

Education is designed to prepare people to live in modern societies. By the standards of primitive man the cultures of such societies *are* artificial and unnatural. Stone-age people did not have to be greatly concerned with numeracy or literacy. They were not often in situations where it would have been obviously useful to make use of elaborate plans or strategies for learning. The contents of today's schooling would not have had much direct value for their everyday lives. For such people, separating learning from doing and confronting them with tasks in which learning and remembering were goals in themselves would not have been at all useful. It would not have helped them to live their daily lives.

But the modern world is different. It *is* useful and necessary for us to be literate and numerate. We need to be literate in order to have satisfactory lives in the culture we find ourselves living in. We also need to be numerate: otherwise everyday tasks that we take for granted like shopping for food and clothes would create serious problems. In order to gain job and leisure skills and vocational qualifications we need to equip ourselves with learning abilities that involve making use of deliberate strategies and plans. School learning is certainly removed from the kinds of learning that are most essential for humans in their natural condition, if by 'natural' we refer to the conditions that existed before the emergence of civilizations. But modern human culture is different. Education in schools needs to be in tune with the realities of life today.

There is always an alternative danger, that the content of school education will become increasingly removed from the concerns of the world outside school. This tendency, wittily parodied 40 years ago in a book called *The Sabre-Tooth Curriculum* (Benjamin, 1939) is ever-present, especially when the world is changing fast.

The Transition to School

The realistic and practical way of responding to the fact that much of the learning that takes place in school is inevitably very different from the kinds of learning that children experience before they start school is to do all that is possible to prepare children for those aspects of school learning that are new and unfamiliar. Of course, teachers of young children are aware of the need for such preparation, and they make considerable efforts in this direction. Thus, for instance, classroom life for beginning students is usually informal. Concrete materials such as blocks and pictures are introduced to help children acquire the basic groundwork for skills which, at a later stage, will depend upon abstract and symbolic forms of thinking.

However, a number of factors combine to make the transition from learning at home to learning at school particularly troublesome, at least for some children. One problem, which can be remedied, is that a teacher who is aware that children do face changes and new challenges when they begin formal schooling may fail to appreciate the magnitude of the changes, or the extent to which children have to become able to deal with unfamiliar learning tasks. Learning to learn as a deliberate activity is not easy. As we saw in chapter 3, the child who enters school may need to be taught even the simplest learning strategies, such as straightforward kinds of rehearsal. Considerable practice may be necessary before the child comes to acquire the regular *habit* of using rehearsal whenever it can help him to learn. Unless the teacher has a fairly clear idea of how to help young children learn to learn in the classroom, some children will remain at a disadvantage which can be just as severe in its effects as unidentified deafness or defective vision.

Another difficulty is that however fully the teacher may be aware of the difficulties to be overcome by the child in meeting new challenges and acquiring new skills and habits needed for success as a learner at school, the practical facilities that are available may be inadequate. Perhaps the biggest problem lies in the sheer scarcity of teachers in an average classroom. When children begin school they are often not used to learning 'on their own', without considerable assistance from an adult. At home there is almost always someone to turn to for assistance with a new or difficult task. A child who suddenly finds himself in a classroom where there is only one teacher to be shared with a large number of other children may feel alarmed and insecure.

However capable the classrom teacher, the sheer numbers of children may make it impossible to give each child the amount of time and attention needed to ensure that every individual learns how to learn in the ways that lead to successful school achievements. The kind of dialogue between one child and a responsive adult which often takes place at home, and which is a valuable source of early learning, particularly in connection with acquiring language, is usually not possible at school. So far as young children are concerned the traditional school classroom is not an ideal environment for learning.

Preparation for learning at school

Compounding the difficulty of adjusting to school is the fact that children vary considerably in the extent to which their experiences at home will have prepared them for the demands of school. Some children enter school well equipped with skills that will be useful in school and experienced in attending to instructions and concentrating on tasks similar to ones they will encounter in the classroom. Such children are typically the offspring of parents who are knowledgeable about educational matters, aware of their children's intellectual needs, and effective at giving instruction and encouraging young learners. Often these children will also have encountered some form of pre-school education outside the home in an environment which shares some features with the school classroom.

Other children will arrive at school poorly prepared. Their early lives may have included fewer of the experiences that prepare an individual for school learning. Their parents may have been relatively inexpert in communicating appropriate skills, unaware of effective ways for helping the child make the transition to school, and perhaps lacking confidence in their ability to perform a teaching function successfully. Some parents may even feel that all matters that concern school are best left to the teachers. Sadly, it is not unknown for school authorities to encourage such attitudes.

Faced with some enormous differences between young children in their preparedness for learning in the school environment, and ill-equipped with either the time or the facilities for giving proper attention to the least well-prepared, it is all too easy for a teacher to label certain pupils as 'slow learners', or even to reach the conclusion that some children are simply incapable of learning in the classroom. For practical purposes, in a classroom with too many children for the teacher to be able to give much attention to the differing needs of each individual, that may be a fairly realistic view of the situation.

If it is not possible to provide opportunities for needy children to gain the mental skills and capacities that school learning depends upon, such children are likely to remain disadvantaged. The tragedy is that such a disadvantage comes about not because these children cannot learn, but simply because the circumstances of their early lives have been ones which have failed to equip them with experiences in the particular forms of learning that (too suddenly, in the case of these pupils) become important when a child first goes to school.

Learning and Child Development

The relationship between learning and child development has given rise to a certain amount of confusion. Ask yourself the question, 'Why do fifteen-year-olds outperform five-year-olds at most learning tasks?' A very common reply is 'Because they are older'.

In the above instance the concept of human development is introduced as an explanation of age-related changes in ability. It is certainly true that older individuals do perform better than young children at most cognitive tasks, and it is equally valid to state that older people are more developed, compared with young children, in various ways. But is it correct to regard development as being the *cause* of age-related improvements?

Maturation

For the young infant, it is undeniably true that many important age-related changes and increases in abilities are related to physiological maturation, that is to say, growth and tissue differentiation, rather than by experience. For example, in some areas of the brain the process known as 'myelinization', whereby parts of the nerves become covered with a fatty tissue that increases the capacity of the nerves to conduct impulses, thus transmitting information, is incomplete at the time of birth. Myelinization, which is essential for some kinds of learning, is completed when the child is around two years of age. Clearly, for a child to make progress towards acquiring those capacities for which myelinization is a pre-condition developmental changes involving physiological maturation must have taken place. Experience alone is insufficient.

Similarly, throughout the first year or two of life many of the child's emerging abilities depend to some extent upon maturation.

However intensively the young child is taught, numerous achievements ranging from the acquisition of perceptual abilities to everyday skills such as walking and climbing stairs cannot be gained until certain developmental processes involving maturation have occurred.

In the above instances development might legitimately be regarded as being a *cause* of age-related changes in the young child. However, by the age of five or six years the maturational processes underlying learning and the achievement of intellectual abilities are largely complete. From around this age, while it is quite permissible to use the term 'development' for *describing* the child's progress, it is less satisfactory to regard development as being the *cause* of the child's continuing advances.

Replying 'because he is older' to the question why an older individual is more successful at some task than a younger child is not particularly helpful. It is an inadequate answer because it does not specify what it is about being older that accounts for the older individual's superior performance. It appears to imply that the cause of improvement lies in some developmental process that is closely linked with age. As we have seen, it is realistic to write in this way about some of the changes that occur in the earliest years of life, but it is wrong to regard development as a cause of changes in later years.

Age and ability

As children get older, they are increasingly likely to make use of strategies and learning plans that add to the effectiveness of school learning. To some extent the increased use of strategies can be seen as reflecting the increasing requirements of school learning, but it can also be seen as partly caused by experiences encountered in schooling. Whatever the reasons, there are substantial increases in the use of elaborative strategies by school children as their age increases, the 'shift' being most marked amongst children in the region of five to seven years of age.

In addition to using strategies increasingly, students acquire *metamemory* skills. These relate to the monitoring and control of one's memory abilities. The child with advanced metamemory skills is good at knowing when it is appropriate to use a strategy, choosing an appropriate strategy for a particular task, applying (or 'transferring') familiar strategies to unfamiliar situations, and accurately estimating her own capacity to retain new information.

So far as school-age children are concerned, citing development as being the explanation of improvements in, say, learning or remembering does not really help to explain anything. Saying that development is the cause of an increase in a child's performance is rather like saying that the cause lies in the passing of time. In fact, of course, time as such causes nothing: it merely provides a medium in which those events that *do* cause changes can occur (Belmont, 1978).

It is hardly surprising that many human attributes are related to age, since the older a person is the larger is the number of opportunities for events that can cause them. Hence, the older a person is the more likely it is that he or she will have, at some time, got drunk, had measles, eaten oysters or moved home. But while the probability of each of these events having occurred is related to a person's age, it is obvious that neither age as such nor development is the direct cause of any of them.

The same kind of reasoning is partly applicable to many age-related changes in learned capacities. The relationship between age and performance on a learning or memory task is not quite so incidental as that between age and the probability of having moved home or eaten oysters, if only because learning is cumulative. It builds upon what has already been learned. As we have seen, many of the things that people learn depend to some extent on previously learned mental activities or previously acquired knowledge: you cannot master advanced algebra until you have some skill at simple arithmetic. Nevertheless, there are good reasons for saying that the differences in mental abilities between the average five-year-old and the average fifteen-year-old do not depend upon strictly developmental processes as such. The disparities in their abilities, whilst *related* to the passing of time, are not *caused* by factors that are closely tied to age. By virtue of their greater age, fifteen-year-olds have had considerably more time than younger children in which to gain knowledge and mental skills. But that is not to say that, *if* young children were taught the necessary knowledge and appropriate mental skills, they would not be capable of performing at the level of fifteen-year-olds.

In practice, age-related differences in young people's abilities are important enough, even if they are the outcome of learning and specific experiences rather than deep-rooted developmental processes. But acknowledging the fact that the older person's advantages are learned ones does have some important practical implications. If we do so, we cannot continue to say that the reason for Jack's failure at algebra is 'because he is not old enough' or that Jane cannot learn to read because she is insufficiently mature, with the implication that all the teacher can do is to wait for the right time to come.

If young children are consistently failing at tasks that give older children no trouble, it is at least worth trying to discover *how* successful older children perform the tasks, and teaching young children to follow the procedures that older individuals draw upon. As we discovered in chapter 3, a strategy of this kind was very successful in raising the level of performance by mentally retarded adolescents at a memory task. Similarly, teaching young children to rehearse was effective in increasing their remembering to the level attained by older children who already rehearsed spontaneously.

Stage theories and alternative approaches

There is every reason to believe that a substantial number of the mental skills, strategies, methods and procedures that older people draw upon to their advantage can fairly readily be acquired by young children, if they are given suitable instruction. A number of instances were described in chapter 3. There is no reason at all to justify teachers being pessimistic or fatalistic about what can be expected on the part of young children. The idea that mental capacities are determined by rigid age-related limits is not supported by hard evidence.

Not all developmental psychologists agree with this point of view. Some would argue that it is inconsistent with the 'stage' theory advanced by Piaget. According to this theory, the structures in the brain that underlie the mental operations which are necessary for reasoning, learning, and solving problems that demand thinking advance through a series of stages. That is to say, at the level of such mental structures, developmental change occurs in steps, in the way we would associate with moving up a staircase as opposed to proceeding along a steady upward slope. According to some developmental psychologists, a child's achievements are limited by the stage he has reached: if a particular ability is one which requires that the child has reached a more advanced stage, there is no point in trying to teach that skill on its own, until the necessary stage has been reached. Moreover, it is argued by some developmental psychologists in the Piagetian tradition that advancing from one stage to another cannot readily be achieved through specific instances of learning: a broad variety of experiences is necessary.

Opposing this point of view is a large body of evidence showing that young children *can* learn many things which, if all the above statements about stages in mental development were correct, they would not be able to learn. For example, Charles Brainerd (1977) has provided considerable hard data to show that the acquisition of concepts that involve a transition from one of Piaget's stages to a higher stage can be achieved by normal learning mechanisms. So long as necessary prerequisite skills are either available to a child or can be taught, there no fundamental reasons, Brainerd argues, why a child cannot learn the abilities which Piaget considered to denote a higher stage of mental development.

Although the contribution of Piaget to our understanding of child development is still very highly regarded, many psychologists now believe that the progress of young children is not so closely linked to fixed stages as followers of Piaget have claimed. Research studies have shown that certain failures by young children at various tasks of reasoning, which were once thought to provide evidence for the existence of definite stages, are actually due to other causes, such as inability to understand the language used in instructions, or failure to see the point of a question. In a number of experiments, when the situation has been modified in such a way as to ensure that the child definitely understands the instructions, and perceives the task as being a meaningful and interesting one, it has been found that young children are indeed capable of performing the mental operations that the task was designed to assess. Some of this research is described in a very readable short book on children's thinking by Margaret Donaldson (1978).

The two viewpoints each have their adherents, but the balance of recent evidence favours those who believe that children's progress at learning and thinking is *not* tightly constrained by rigid stages. As early as 1968, R. M. Gagne suggested that it ought to be possible to teach any child a relatively advanced skill, as long as it is possible to ensure that the child is taught each of the successively more difficult sub-skills that lead the child from his existing level of competence towards achieving the skill in question.

In practice, of course, this may be impossible in the time that is available. In theory, it may well be possible to begin teaching a three-year-old the skills required by a nuclear physicist, but the child will be considerably older than three by the time much progress has been made! Nevertheless, emphasizing the learned quality of virtually all of the intellectual skills gained after early childhood helps to put our ideas about learning and abilities into the proper perspective. There is no inescapable limitation in young children that makes it completely impossible for them to gain learned abilities that are usually achieved by older children. There are few firm limits on what a child can learn.

However young and inexperienced the child, it is rarely wise to leap to the conclusion that gaining some desired skill is impossible: it is always worth trying to enable the child to acquire it. It is often the case that much additional knowledge or many intervening skills must be learned before the desired achievements can be made, but that is no excuse for sitting back and leaving things to the imagined effects of maturation or the progress of time.

6

Abilities and the Individual Student

No two learners are the same: every person is unique. This awkward fact of life causes difficulties in the classroom, and schools and educational systems vary enormously in the ways in which they take individual differences into account.

It is sometimes useful to categorize students on the basis of factors related to their success at school. Pupils may be described as being more or less *able*, of having greater or less *aptitude* for a task, or as being relatively *fast* or *slow learners*. The assessment is usually done by some kind of test, designed to ensure that it is *objective* in the sense that the scores are not influenced by subjective judgements made by teachers or others. Such tests can be valuable for the teacher, if they accurately predict individual success. However, there is always a danger that tests will be misused, or their findings misapplied, and a number of scientists have argued that any practical gains from ability testing are outweighed by the destructive effects resulting from abuse of the tests.

Intelligence and Ability

The most ambitious tests, and the most controversial, are the ones designed to measure *intelligence*. Intelligence-testing goes back to the beginning of the present century, and it has been extensively used for selection purposes within education. Although intelligence-test scores are not particularly effective for predicting accurately how individuals will fare at particular educational experiences, such scores do give a useful global indication of general intellectual ability, and one that is fairly highly correlated with school achievement.

How is intelligence measured? Many scientific concepts are defined in precise terms which specify the operations necessary for objectively measuring them. Accordingly, in order to discover how to measure temperature in degrees centigrade or distance in metres one simply needs to know how these terms are defined.

This is not possible with the psychological concept of intelligence. It has not proved possible to define intelligence in terms that show precisely how it is to be measured. Definitions vary: most psychologists who have used the word would agree that it refers to a person's intellectual abilities, but disagreements crowd in as soon as one starts to be more precise. The well-known statement that 'intelligence is what intelligence tests measure' may not be particularly helpful to teachers interested in assessing their students' abilities, but it is accurate in its way, and it warns us not to expect too much guidance from any definition of intelligence.

Intelligence as a possible cause of high achievement

Intelligence tests measure a person's ability to answer certain questions that require intellectual skills not unlike ones that are taught in school. Consequently, if the scores of a group of students at a test of intelligence are compared with ratings of the same students' academic success at school, the relationship between the two sets of scores, or *correlation*, will be quite high. It might be claimed that the existence of such a relationship proves that school success is *caused* by high intelligence. However, the relationship can be explained equally well by the fact that the intelligence test scores and the other indications of academic success are based on measures of performance at similar tasks. Essentially, the same skills are being measured.

The contents of an intelligence test are determined not by any precise definition of intelligence, but by the judgement of whoever writes the questions about what constitutes intelligence. Consequently, the choice of questions, and hence the composition of the test, will inevitably reflect the view of the individual who constructs the questions about what constitutes human intelligence. Another factor that will be taken into account in deciding which questions to include is the relationship between people's performance on those questions and their performance at other tests designed to measure intelligence and other abilities.

It follows that if students' performance on a particular new question or set of questions is closely related to their performance on other questions that have been used in intelligence tests, the former question is likely to be considered to be a good one for measuring intelligence. Thus a student's intelligence-test score might be defined as being a measure of the performance of that person at questions measuring those aspects of intellectual ability that are considered to be important by whoever designed the test and by the designers of other intelligence tests.

A definition of this kind reminds us that intelligence, as measured, is not an absolute or fixed quantity, nor is it a fundamental cause of a person's achievements. However objective the testing procedure, the element of subjectivity that is present when tests are designed precludes this. Nevertheless, if an easily administered intelligence test provides scores which effectively predict how well an individual will succeed at, say, a new job, or a training course, or a school-based course of instruction, the test will undoubtedly be useful for teachers and others. So long as educators who make use of test scores for practical purposes avoid the very common error of overestimating the accuracy with which intelligence test scores can actually predict future achievements, the practical benefits can be considerable.

Intelligence tests can be a convenient means of gaining a broad indication of a person's performance at a range of tasks requiring intellectual skills. But it is only too easy to fall into the habit of regarding intelligence, as measured in an intelligence test, as being the cause of a person's success or lack of success. For example, a person who does well at school and also gains a high score in an intelligence test is said to have done well because he is intelligent. Such a statement is not objectionable if by 'intelligence' one is simply referring to the dictionary definition, although there is an element of circular reasoning involved. It is rather like saying that a person performed well at a task because he the kind of person who does well at tasks of this kind.

The statement that a person did well because he is intelligent is more objectionable, however, if it is meant to imply that intelligence as measured is the cause of good performance at various other tasks. In that case, the underlying reasoning is rather like that involved in saying that a light meter causes the day to grow dark. Undoubtedly, a light meter may provide a good *measure* of the amount of light, and the reading on the meter will be closely related to alternative indications of how light it is at any time. But the fact that fluctuations in light, however assessed, are closely related to changes in light meter recordings is clearly no basis for suggesting that the meter is the cause of fluctuations in lighting. If people in a primitive society fell into such an error we might well laugh at them, and regard their fallacious deduction as being an indication of primitive reasoning. However, with regard to intelligence we are very prone to make exactly the same error ourselves.

Intelligence and Learning

It is widely believed that intelligence is a good measure of ability to learn. We assume that an intelligent person must be good at learning. Indeed, certain definitions of intelligence state this explicitly. In fact, the evidence is that correlations between measures of intelligence and measures of learning are very low: knowing a person's score on an intelligence test does not lead to accurate predictions of that person's performance on a learning task.

There are a number of reasons for this. One is that a person who is good at one kind of learning may have less success at other forms of learning. Playing football and programming computers are two skills that depend heavily on learning, but being good at one of them does not lead to high levels of performance on the other skill. In one study, a number of children aged five were each given eleven different tests of learning and memory (Stevenson, Parker and Wilkinson, 1975). After the tests had been scored, the experimenters computed the correlations between each child's scores on all 11 tests. These were found to be very low, averaging +.14. Correlations of this size are virtually useless for making predictions about an individual child's scores. Therefore, knowing that a particular child performed well (or badly) at one of the tasks of learning and remembering does not help us to predict how that child would fare on the other tasks.

Even psychologists who are firmly committed to the use of intelligence tests admit that there is no straightforward relationship between learning and measured intelligence. For example, Jensen (1978) notes that the correlations between measures of performance at a large number of simple learning tasks are meagre, and that the correlations between performance at learning tasks and scores on intelligence tests are also very small.

Despite the evidence, many people cling to the view that each person has a fixed capacity to learn, and that this capacity is closely related to intelligence. The fact that intelligence test scores are related to a person's learned *achievements* encourages us to believe that intelligence and learning must be closely connected. However, in investigations involving very simple forms of learning that are 'uncontaminated' by most of the broader influences that lead to some people being more successful as learners than others, such as previous knowledge, attentiveness, differences in motivation, the use of deliberate strategies, for example, it has been found that systematic differences in learning rate are remarkable only for their absence (Estes, 1970). Even when normal and mentally retarded individuals are compared, consistent differences in learning rates at tasks of 'pure' learning are hard to find.

Nor has it proved possible to identify any measure of learning rate that is basic to all kinds of learning. It used to be widely thought (Thorndike, 1931) that learning capacity depends upon the number of nerve connections that are available for forming new associations between items to be learned. A related view was that learning rate depended upon the speed with which information could be transmitted along networks of nerves: good learners were supposed to transmit information faster than slow learners. However, no firm evidence has been obtained to support theories of this kind. Moreover, as we pointed out in chapter 1, physiological research has failed to identify any one kind of underlying physical event or 'engram' that is common to every form of learning.

Undoubtedly, some people are more successful than others at particular learning tasks: in that sense it is realistic to speak of 'good learners' and 'poor learners'. But it would be wrong to assume that the differences between such people are caused by fundamental differences in the rates at which they are capable of learning.

A major limitation of intelligence tests is that they do little to describe in any detail *how* people vary in intelligence, let alone help explain *why* people differ in intellectual ability. An intelligence test score is broadly analogous to a measure of productivity. It may be useful to speak of one factory being more productive than another, and a readily obtained index of productivity may be extremely valuable. But when it comes to comparing different factories, or asking why one produces more goods than another, it is not at all helpful to be told that the reason is 'because the factory is more productive'!

The above analogy is slightly unfair to intelligence tests, because it is usual for test scores to be provided in the form of a profile which indicates the level of performance on each of a number of components of the test. Consequently, it is normally possible to discern whether a person performs better at, say, verbal tasks or spatial tasks. Nevertheless, intelligence test scores are not very informative about the reasons underlying a high or low level of performance. They do little to identify the causes of an individual's weaknesses, or to indicate the particular skills or abilities that a person would need to acquire in order to gain higher scores in the future. The failure to provide such information may contribute to perpetuating the largely erroneous view that the abilities measured by intelligence tests are fixed and unvarying capacities.

Hereditary Determinants of Human Abilities

Although scores on tests of intelligence are not highly correlated with measures of learning rate at particular tasks, measures of people's intelligence are undoubtedly related to their learned achievements.

One reason for this apparently paradoxical state of affairs is that even in the absence of any fundamental variability in learning rate, in practical circumstances the extensiveness of an individual's acquired skills and abilities will depend upon various other factors that influence learning in one way or another. These include, in addition to motivational influences and differences in attentiveness and in the use of effective learning strategies, additional determinants of learning such as individual differences in perception, in perseverence, in impulsivity, and a number of temperamental variables, and a person's existing knowledge and skills. Since the latter have a cumulative, 'snowballing' influence upon the individual's learned achievements, it naturally follows that previous learning will affect a person's degree of success at new learning tasks, even in the absence of any differences in the (narrowly defined) rate of learning.

There is strong evidence that inherited factors contribute to measured intelligence, and it is highly likely that hereditary influences also have effects on learning, direct or indirect. But most of the evidence that indicates existence of relationships between hereditary factors and human abilities is in the form of observed correlations. These simply show that some relationship exists: they provide little indication concerning *why*, and they give no proof that a cause-and-effect link is involved. Precisely *how* intelligence is affected by genetics – the complex instructions that are transmitted via the chromosomes – remains a mystery. To complicate matters, it is established that when human characteristics are known to be caused by genetic factors, the precise ways in which genetic influences have their effects are rarely simple: typically, lengthy and complicated chains of interacting processes are involved.

Very little is known about the manner in which genetically transmitted influences affect learning. There are numerous possibilities. Conceivably, genetic factors might exert their effects via any one or any combination of the numerous factors that can affect learning. We are even in the dark concerning whether learning is affected relatively directly or only indirectly, via influences such as perception or attentiveness.

Genetics and learning

There has been much research into the question of whether, and by how much, people's achievements are affected by genetically transmitted information. But from a practical point of view it is much more important to know about the manner in which genetic factors exert their influence. Until we have such knowledge, our awareness of the implications for school learning of genetic effects, however large or small, will remain extremely vague. When we do find out how genetic factors contribute to individual differences in learned achievements, we will be much closer to knowing what to do in order to bring about practical increases in people's achievements at learned abilities.

Hereditability. A great deal of controversy surrounds research into the influence of hereditary factors on human achievements. Some researchers, including Hans Eysenck and Arthur Jensen, consider that it is valuable to estimate the *hereditability* of intelligence. This gives an indication of the degree to which intelligence is inherited in a given population. Typically, hereditability is assessed by methods which are based on making comparisons between the correlations of scores obtained by identical twins and non-identical twins.

Other researchers have objected that the validity of such methods rests on certain questionable assumptions, such as that the experiences of identical twins are no more similar than those of other twins. They point to various complications, including the fact that the more uniform the environment the higher the estimate of hereditability. It has also been suggested that apportioning values to the relative influences of environmental and hereditary influences on human traits such as learning wrongly implies they are distinct and separate forces that can be simply added together or multiplied. Geneticists have pointed out that the ways in which the influences of genetic and environmental forces combine together are actually exceedingly complicated. Therefore, it is argued,

> It is nonsense to speculate that observed levels of IQ for individuals or groups of individuals are mostly innate because the heritability of the trait may be high. To support this kind of judgement, every possible genotype would have to be raised in every possible environment. . . . Then and only then could we make definitive statements about the relative effects of environment and hereditability. (McGuire and Hirsch, 1977, p. 68)

A particular problem is that the validity of the hereditability measure depends upon certain conditions being met, notably that hereditary and environmental influences act independently of one another. This state of affairs does exist in circumstances to which the hereditability measure has traditionally been applied, such as plant growth. There, the action of environmental factors (soil characteristics, temperature, rainfall, and so on) is relatively independent of genetic influences. In human lives, however, hereditary and environmental factors are not independent. This has various consequences. For example, monozygotic (genetically identical) infant twins who look alike become more similar in temperament than monozygotic twins whose appearance is dissimilar. A probable cause of this finding is that adults confuse twins who appear virtually identical with one another. The result is a reduction in the differences in people's responses to the two children, which leads to greater similarity in the twins' environmental experiences.

Quite apart from these complications, there are contradictions which are not easily resolved in the evidence concerning possible hereditary influences on intelligence. A number of findings appear to contradict the view that the hereditability of intelligence is

relatively high. When opportunities for environmental and hereditary factors to work together are ruled out, estimates of the hereditability of intelligence (obtained from examining test scores of
people who are genetically related to one another) are considerably
reduced. For example, in studies based on measures of people for
whom blood group gives the only indication of genetic make up,
the correlations between intelligence-test scores and genetic measures are much lower than they are in circumstances where genetic
indicators, such as skin colour, can affect the environmental factors
in a person's early life. Very low measures of hereditability are
obtained from data based on the intelligence-test scores of children
who are the offspring of black and white American GIs, but who
were brought up in Europe without their natural fathers, thus
eliminating the usual opportunities for environmental and genetic
factors to act together (Loehlin, Vandenberg and Osborne, 1973).

The Environment

In many of the studies that have examined the influences of hereditary and environmental factors upon human achievements it has
been assumed that a person's 'environment' can be readily
measured. In fact, when we stop to think about what is actually
meant by this word, it is clear that the concept of an environment is
not so simple as it first appears to be. We think of the term
environment as referring to that part of the world outside an
individual that influences the person. But a person can only be
influenced by those elements of the external world to which he or
she is sensitive, that is, elements that are detected or perceived by
that person.

A blind man may be in a room filled with beautiful pictures, but
because he cannot see them the pictures will not form part of his
experience. For similar reasons, any attempt to measure or assess
objectively the characteristics of a person's environment is suspect.
The environment that influences an individual is not the the same as
the environment as described by others: it is the environment as
uniquely perceived and experienced by that particular individual.
As the Swedish psychologist Ference Marton has pointed out, differences in how individuals experience the world and 'interpret'
learning situations have important educational implications

(Marton, 1981). Furthermore, perception and learning are also influenced by the *personality* of the individual student (Biggs and Telfer, 1981; Entwistle and Cunningham, 1968; Fontana, 1981).

In practice, since most humans share perceptual capacities, and since many people have knowledge that is held in common with others, their perceptions of an event may be similar. When a group of children are told to look in the direction of a nearby tree and state what they can see, each child may report seeing a tree. But even in this instance, as soon as we start to ask the children about further aspects of their experience (for example, asking 'What is the significance of this tree? What does it mean to you?') it becomes clear that different individuals' experiences of an ostensibly uniform environment can be extremely varied.

Hence, although it is certainly true to say that children are influenced by their environments, it is wrong to assume that what a particular child will learn depends on properties of the environment that can be objectively specified by any other person. Each person's experiences of an environment are unique and constantly subject to variation, largely because people learn from their own experiences. Many factors connected with individual development and learning, including perceptual sensitivity, personality and temperament, combine together to ensure that however uniform an environment might appear to be, people's actual experiences differ very considerably. It is quite impossible for objective measurement of a human environment to give a precise indication of what is actually experienced by a particular individual.

Adding to the difficulty of assessing the important features of any person's environment is the fact that individual qualities not only affect a person's experiences of environmental events, but they also influence the environment itself. For example those environmental events that are provided by a mother's behaviour towards her child are greatly affected by the child's own activities.

These problems have not prevented psychologists from doing all they can to assess the important properties of children's environments. Observational techniques that are used in recent research show great ingenuity in trying to go well beyond simple ratings of the properties of a child's world, and attempting to measure whatever the child actually experiences. Simple environmental measures that were used in the past, such as the number of books in a child's home, have been replaced by much more sophisticated procedures, such as analyses of the interactional sequences of the mother and young child as they respond to each other.

In attempts to examine and compare the effects of hereditary and environmental influences upon human abilities, the fact that the experiences which children's environments generate influence them in ways that are too diverse and too complicated to be readily measured may lead to environmental influences being underestimated. An analogy will help to clarify this point. Imagine that you want to compare the effects of temperature and rainfall on the growth of plants. If your measure of the amount of rainfall is very accurate and your measure of temperature is a very imprecise one, the result will be seriously to overestimate the effect of rainfall and underestimate that of temperature. As a rule, if something cannot be properly measured, the chances are that its influence will be underestimated.

Another factor that may have caused the effects of environments to be underestimated in the past is that, owing to people's lack of knowledge about those aspects of a child's environment that are most important for human learning, some of the most crucial aspects of children's environments may have varied relatively little. As we gain more knowledge about the environmental factors that make the largest contributions to what a child actually learns, and it becomes possible to produce environments for learning that are increasingly effective, the effective range of variability of environmental quality will also increase. An effect of this may be to increase the contribution of environmental influences to measured intelligence and to human achievements.

Early Individual Differences

Everyone agrees that, as learners, children are very different from one another by the time they begin school. It is not always realized how deep-rooted are some of the individual factors that influence what a child learns. In fact, differences between children in a number of attributes that affect learning can be seen as early as the first year of life.

Research with infants (Korner, 1971) has revealed that a variety of individual differences between infants, affecting either their activities or their perceptual abilities, can affect later experience and learning. For example, as soon as they are born, some infants cry more than others. Crying acts to bring about social contacts between mother and infant, and consequently differences between babies in their crying behaviour can influence caretaking by the mother and the accompanying social interactions. As a result, early social learning will be affected. Also, babies react differently to being soothed and picked up when they are crying. Some remain comforted for a long time: others soon require more attention. Differences in the way babies respond to caretaking may influence how mothers respond to their children. For instance, an inexperienced mother's feelings of competence may be strongly affected by the reactions to her attempts to soothe the baby. In turn, her feelings of success or failure may affect her actions in the future as she interacts with the child in the situations that determine the form of the child's earliest social learning.

Another early difference that can have a big influence on what a child learns is in what some researchers term *cuddliness*. Most babies are cuddly, but some infants do not seem to like being held and resist their mothers' attempts to hug or embrace them. These 'non-cuddlers' dislike physical constraints of any kind and they are more restless than other infants. Differences in degree of cuddliness inevitably lead to differences in the way infants are handled, and influence the interactions that take place between mother and child (Schaffer and Emerson, 1964). The formation of social attachments may also be affected adversely. However, for those kinds of learning that involve limb movements, non-cuddlers have an advantage, resulting from their restlessness and high level of physical activity.

Individual differences in infants' perceptual sensitivity are a further cause of early differences in learning. Some infants seem to require more sensory stimulation that others. Babies who need a large amount of stimulation are described as having a high *visual threshold*. More sensitive infants, with lower visual thresholds, are overwhelmed and made anxious by too much sensory stimulation.

The effects of differences in perceptual sensitivity may combine with those of early social differences, as in the following sequence of events. Young infants who cry often are frequently picked up. When infants are picked up they tend to become visually attentive, and gain experience of the visual world. Those infants who have high visual thresholds, who benefit from having extra visual stimulation, stand to gain more from the experience of being picked up than the more sensitive infants with low visual thresholds. For the latter, the effect of picking them up frequently may be to upset them by over-stimulation: they may receive all the visual stimulation they need without being picked up. In consequence, young infants will be affected in differing ways when their mothers pick them up. Conversely, some of the effects of maternal neglect, for instance when a mother does not regularly pick up and play with her child, will be more severe for a child who has a high threshold than for a child who has more visual sensitivity. Children with a high visual threshold will be more adversely affected by not being picked up.

Such early differences can have long-lasting effects. For example, it has been found that infants who are physically active often become five-year-olds with higher scores on tests of motor performance than on tests of verbal achievement (Escalona, 1973). It was also found that five-year-old children who as infants were rated as being highly sensitive are good at communicating sensitively and precisely. These findings add weight to the view that in order to assess the effects of environmental factors upon a child it is essential to know something about the way the individual *experiences* the events in his life.

Critical Periods

For many reasons, the first few years of life are extremely important for later development. A number of authors have expressed this view in a more extreme form, and have stated that the earliest years are so crucial that if certain skills are not acquired then, the child will be at a serious disadvantage throughout life.

So far as the acquisition of a child's first language is concerned, this may be true. But for most other kinds of learning the evidence indicates that it would be an exaggeration to state that certain early periods of a child's life are absolutely 'critical'. Generally, if skills are not acquired at the normal time they can be learned later. It has been found that children who have become retarded as a result of appalling neglect and deprivation may regain most if not all of the lost ground if they receive intense stimulation and instruction in later years (Clarke and Clarke, 1976). Of course, there may be major advantages to learning something early in life. For example, some aspects of learning a second language may be much easier for a child who is too young to feel self-conscious about speaking in an unfamiliar tongue.

Although the evidence does not support the view that there are definite critical periods for human learning, and shows that there is great flexibility in the ways in which development can take place, the sequencing of a child's experiences is crucial. A number of training studies have shown that timing and phasing of learning is highly important. For example, Burton White (1971), who studied the progress of infants towards gaining the ability to reach out for objects and pick them up, observed that what appears to be a simple feat depends upon the precise co-ordination of a number of sub-skills. White was interested in the possibility of accelerating babies' progress by providing an 'enriched' environment, but his first efforts were unsuccessful. He knew that visual attending was one important sub-skill, and he knew from previous work that showing infants bright visual objects would improve their attending skills. However, White found to his surprise that the effect of the visual stimuli he provided was to delay rather than accelerate the infants' acquisition of reaching skills. Subsequently, however, he discovered that he had mistakenly provided enrichment at an inappropriate time. His visual stimuli had encouraged the babies to look at the displays at a period in life when they would normally spend a good deal of time looking at their hands. For the young infant, looking at one's own hands is a very good way of starting to learn to integrate visual activities and hand movements, a form of co-ordination which is essential for picking up objects. In effect, White's enriching materials had retarded learning, not because they were ineffective but because they came at the wrong time, and interfered with the acquisition of essential skills.

These and other findings show that a child's achievements at learning new skills will be strongly influenced by whether or not new skills have been introduced at appropriate times and in a logical order. Researchers have introduced terms such as *optimum stimulation* and *the optimum match* to indicate the importance of trying to mesh environmental stimulation with individual children's particular abilities and needs.

Early Experience

There was at one time a fairly widespread view that a child's eventual achievements were almost entirely determined by events in the first few years of life. Such a view rested on a misinterpretation of evidence that showed that the progress of children could be predicted fairly well on the basis of their early childhood achievements. The fallacy lies in the assumption that because mature achievements can be *predicted* at an early age, they must have been *determined* early in life. In fact, one reason why early achievements happen to be a good predictor of later achievements is that early achievements are a good predictor of the environmental *circumstances* in later years.

If a child is brought up during the early years in a loving home with parents who devote effort and expertise to helping the child to become an effective and independent learner, it is very likely that the child will achieve at a high level and it is also likely that the child will continue to receive the same environmental advantages in subsequent years. For similar reasons we might predict that a person who lives at a certain address in 1988 will live at the same address in 1998. The fact that such a prediction may be correct does not prove that living at an address in the earlier year *causes* a person to be at the same address ten years later: it simply reflects the fact that influential conditions prevailing at one period usually continue to have an influence for some time ahead.

The family

Pychologists have conducted a large amount of research designed to investigate the effects of family influences upon children's learning. Not surprisingly, much of the research has focused upon the mother's role. Mothers have an enormous influence upon their children's learning.

As was remarked in chapter 5, learning situations within the family typically involve reciprocal interaction between mother and child on a one-to-one basis. Mother and child engage in conversational dialogues, which in many ways form ideal backgrounds for learning (Wells, 1981). So far as school learning is concerned, the most successful parents are those who have prepared their offspring for learning in the very different circumstances of the classroom, where social conditions are more formal, the content of instruction often more abstract, and the goals of learning less relevant to the immediate demands of everyday life.

As one might expect, young children's intellectual achievements are fairly highly correlated with measures of the abilities of the parents, especially of the mother. This fact is as consistent with a genetic interpretation as it is with one which attaches greater importance to environmental factors, of course. However, it is noteworthy that correlations between young children's abilities and the number of years for which their mothers attended school are higher than the correlations between children's abilities and mothers' intelligence test scores. It seems that the extent to which a child's mother is 'school-wise', in being aware of the special demands of school learning, and competent to prepare her child for school, is extremely important.

Among the numerous activities that take place in interactions between children and those parents who are effective at preparing their children for the kinds of learning tasks that are encountered when the child begins school, interactions with picture books are especially influential. Such interactions can be seen as forming an especially effective kind of adult-child dialogue, in the course of which the mother gives instruction, ask questions and responds to the child in ways that she judges to be appropriate.

It is impossible to overestimate the importance of the family and home for giving the child a grounding in some of the kinds of learning that will be encountered at school. To repeat what was said earlier, all children learn many things irrespective of the particular circumstances of their home backgrounds: the crucial differences, so far as success at school is concerned, lie not in the total amount of knowledge or the number of skills acquired but in the effectiveness of the child's preparation for the special demands of learning at school. This fact raises a number of debatable issues. Should schools do more to help ill-prepared children? Is the school classroom a good learning environment for the immature child? Undoubtedly the present state of affairs is an unfair one, with built-in advantages for the children of communicative, articulate, school-wise middle-class parents. But this state of affairs is an unavoidable fact of life in the closing decades of the twentieth century.

Family size. The amount and quality of interaction between parents and child is to some extent determined by objectively measurable limitations on the time that parents have to devote to each of their children. For this reason, factors such as the number of children in the family and the children's birth order have an effect on children's achievements (Marjoribanks, 1977; Zajonc, 1976). Children's scores on tests of intellectual performance decline as the size of the family increases, as would be expected if parents have a limited amount of time and attention to be shared between their children. Although the decline is greater in families of lower social class, most of the relevant evidence indicates that there is a decline of child performance with family size even when social class is held constant, except amongst particular groups of people, such as Mormons, who think it highly desirable for parents to have a large number of children. In large families the negative relationship between performance and family size is greatest for the children in the middle, a finding which is consistent with the view that the amount of parental attention that is available is important.

Deprivation and Compensation

An enormous amount has been written about deprivation and its effects, and about the successes and failures of the many programmes that have been designed to provide compensatory experiences. The term *deprivation* has been applied somewhat indiscriminately to a range of home circumstances which for one reason or another are not effective for ensuring that the child is ready to take full advantage of school. (In other respects, of course, many of these children may be anything but deprived.)

Interaction with the parent is a key element in preparing the child for school tasks. Conversely, the absence of interactive experiences, especially those in the form of instructional dialogues, is a source of deprivation that may lead to a child being retarded in the skills and knowledge needed for school success. Interactions with adults provide opportunities for the child to focus on particular environmental experiences. At the same time the child receives guidance, selection and feedback to shape, sequence and structure learning (Feuerstein, 1979). In the absence of appropriate kinds of interaction with the parent, these opportunities are lacking.

There are many reasons for parents being unable to interact with their children in the ways that are most beneficial for school learning. Parents may be apathetic, lacking in confidence, ignorant, depressed, tired or overcommitted. The mother may perceive herself as being relatively powerless, and unable to influence her child's education. Such fatalism is not uncommon among people who are poor and uneducated (Howe, 1975). In some sub-cultures, the kind of dialogue-based interaction that is necessary if the parents are to provide a good preparation for school learning may be regarded as alien or even undesirable.

There is considerable controversy about the effectiveness of compensatory programmes designed to provide enriching experiences to help children who are thought to be educationally disadvantaged or deprived. It is certainly true that many of the programmes have failed to produce long-lasting advantages. Some people have argued that such failures demonstrate that all compensatory programmes are doomed to fail. It is more accurate to regard the absence of long-lasting success with some programmes as resulting from unrealistic expectations about the outcomes of interventions that were often relatively brief, not well designed, and administered by teachers who were often inexperienced and sometimes entirely untrained.

Underlying much of the thinking that went into such programmes was the belief that the effects of a brief educational intervention can be analogous to those of an injection which is given in order to immunize a person against some physical disease. In fact the analogy is a false and misleading one. A child's intellectual development cannot be accelerated (or arrested) by any sudden 'shot in the arm'. The factors that lead to a child acquiring a steadily increasing range of abilities are too numerous and complex, and too dependent on the appropriate timing and sequencing of experiences, to be replaced by any quick dose of enrichment.

On the other hand, it is true to say (see chapters 2 and 3) that certain key skills which are quickly acquired, such as the strategy of rehearsing whenever it is useful to do so, can have very widespread benefits for the young child. Moreover, when intervention programmes have taken full account of the magnitude of the task they have usually been successful. Those programmes which were long-lasting, intensive and administered by experienced teachers, which have made provision for considerable interaction between adults and each individual child, and which have involved accurate identification of the necessary skills that children lacked have been highly effective. But with the best compensatory programmes, it would be naive to assume that their effects will inevitably be permanent even when a child subsequently returns to longer-lasting conditions of environmental deprivation: the analogy of a 'shot in the arm' remains an inappropriate one, however large or potent the shot may be.

7

Comprehension: Understanding Stories and Texts

The ability to learn from written materials is amongst the most important of all the skills taught at school. But understanding written information is not easy: it demands the capacity to combine a number of the learning skills that have been described in earlier chapters. Many students leave school with limited expertise in learning from passages of text.

This chapter examines ways of enabling students to increase their understanding, or *comprehension*, of what they read. There are close ties between learning, reading and comprehension. In previous chapters we have looked at some of the methods that learners use to help them understand new materials. Existing knowledge is possibly the most important single factor: people make extensive use of whatever they already know in order to make sense of new information. Such knowledge may be in the form of data about the attributes of a single item or event, or it may take the form of a large schema containing highly organized information about a sequence of events, such as going to a restaurant or travelling on a bus.

A student can do various things to aid understanding. For example, information that is unfamiliar can sometimes be made easier to comprehend by providing a heading or title, as was shown in chapter 4. A title may direct the reader to something that he or she already knows that will clarify the meaning of the new information. Alternatively, as we have seen, when new information cannot readily be connected to existing knowledge, it may be possible to make *advance organizers* which help perform that function. The successful learner is good at finding links between existing knowledge and new materials: becoming able to do so is an important aspect of learning how to learn. Activities such as rehearsal, self-testing and making summaries can all contribute to the effectiveness with which a person introduces existing knowledge in order to assist new learning. And making use of existing knowledge depends upon the learner possessing the necessary *retrieval* skills and being able to apply or *transfer* old skills and knowledge to new circumstances.

Helping Students to Understand

Teachers can do much to improve children's ability to comprehend text, and we shall describe some highly successful training projects. Many researchers have investigated comprehension skills, but only a few investigators have been successful in devising training methods that lead to large and practical gains in students' success at understanding written information. However, relatively simple activities by students can improve some aspects of comprehension. Note-taking, for example, can be helpful, especially when learners express information in their own words rather than copying it word for word (Howe, 1977). Students who undertake study activities such as underlining or taking notes gain more benefit from a period of study than students who are inactive (Brown and Smiley, 1978).

Although the present chapter emphasizes the contributions to comprehension of learners' own activities, it is clear that an individual's understanding of new information will also be influenced by the manner in which it is presented. The importance of the *content* is obvious enough: few ten-year-olds will make sense of a passage from a textbook in advanced physics, because they lack too much of the knowledge necessary for comprehension. But a child's understanding is also affected by the *structure* of prose materials. For example, young children find stories easier to understand if they conform to the familiar, 'well-formed' structure of a traditional tale.

Study activities and the use of existing knowledge go hand in hand. The likelihood of an activity making a useful contribution to learning depends upon the learner's ability to make effective use of what is already known (Brown and Smiley, 1978). These authors found that students only benefited from activities such as note-taking or underlining when they were capable of identifying the important points in the information.

Inserted questions

A tried and tested way to improve a student's understanding of the information in a prose passage is to insert questions in the material. Teachers in the classroom often ask questions, and there are many good reasons for doing so. Numerous research studies have demonstrated the value of questions for improving learning and comprehension of information presented in prose form. Also, the effectiveness of the *programmed learning* systems of instruction that were favoured by educators in the 1960s heavily depended on the fact that students had to respond to frequent questions about the content being taught.

The word *mathemagenics* was introduced by E. Rothkopf (1970) as a general term for study activities that promote learning, such as reading, asking questions, inspecting items, attending to the teacher, and mentally reviewing learned materials. Much of Rothkopf's research has concentrated on examining the effects of encouraging readers to answer questions that are embedded in passages of prose. Questions inserted into text can undoubtedly help students to master the specific information that is tested by the questions.

There is less certainty about the effects of inserted questions on the learning and comprehension of those aspects of a passage that are not specifically tested. Some studies have found definite improvements, others have not. Factors such as the positioning of the questions (in particular, whether a question appears before or after the part of the passage to which it refers) and their number and density are also important. The effects of these additional factors depend upon the content and form of the particular learning material in which they are inserted, and also upon individual matters such as the interest level and the degree of difficulty experienced by the particular learner. Consequently, simple generalizations about their influence are not possible.

Coding and comprehending

Teachers have many ways of helping children to understand materials that are new and unfamiliar. They ask questions, demonstrate their own curiosity, assist children to predict what will happen next in a story, and try to activate children's background knowledge. Teachers also tailor messages to children's own level, question their assumptions, encourage them to make inferences, direct attention to the main points, and force children to make their thoughts and ideas explicit (Brown, Palincsar and Armbruster, 1984).

These authors draw attention to the fact that, for a number of reasons, those young children who need the greatest amount of help in comprehending the materials they read often receive less assistance than children whose early efforts have been more successful. Why is this? One reason is related to the fact that the efforts of teachers to help children learn to understand take place in the context of learning to read: reading and comprehension are inseparable. The evidence shows that those children who make the slowest progress at learning to read, and are relatively unsuccessful, are often given instruction which gives emphasis to the decoding aspects of learning to read rather than to comprehension.

Understandably, teachers who are faced with children who are not well prepared for learning to read, or who are not progressing well and seem to lack basic skills, may decide to give remedial instruction that emphasizes the basic decoding skills that these children lack. Brown and her co-authors note that disadvantaged pupils are often taught to read by instructional programmes that emphasize decoding skills, whereas middle-class children are typically exposed to reading programmes that put more stress on comprehension.

In consequence, differences in children's preparedness for reading when they begin school may lead to differences in the kind of instruction they receive. In particular, disadvantaged and less successful students are taught in ways that give less emphasis to comprehension. Good readers are often made to think about the meaning of the information they are reading. They are frequently asked to criticize passages and evaluate stories. Poor readers, on the other hand, get less practice at reading aloud, partly to avoid the embarrassment of repeated failure. Their reading exercises give more emphasis to pronunciation and decoding.

It is quite understandable that a teacher should decide to give increased emphasis to decoding and other basic skills when a child is making little progress at learning to read. There are good practical reasons for making use of instructional materials in which decoding and related abilities are stressed, particularly for children who are failing to progress at the normal rate. Unfortunately, however, the resulting reduction in the time and effort that is spent helping these children to acquire comprehension skills tends to increase their problems with understanding what they read. These students may learn some important reading skills but they are handicapped in learning how to learn *from* reading.

The Skills of Comprehension

What does a child have to do in order to comprehend written information, and how can this be taught? Some of the more important component skills have been described by Allan Collins and Edward Smith (1982). These authors commence by stating that if cognitive psychologists can specify in sufficient detail the processes that underlie thinking skills it will then be possible to devise effective methods for teaching students to master the skills. Collins and Smith next attempt to specify *what* people need to learn, if they are to comprehend passages of prose. Basically, two kinds of comprehension skills have to be acquired.

The first group of skills are *comprehension-monitoring* abilities. The reader invokes these skills in order to keep a check on his ongoing comprehension processes as he reads, to be aware when they break down, and to take some effective action to remedy the situation whenever they do so.

The second category of comprehension skills contains ones that are necessary for *hypothesis formation and evaluation*. These underlie a student's ability to use various items of information in the text as clues for making hypotheses about what is happening or predictions about what is coming next (for example, 'X is going to rob the bank'). As new evidence arrives from the material that is being read, the reader evaluates the hypotheses and predictions. If they turn out to be wrong they can be adjusted or revised. Collins and Smith make a distinction between the two activities of hypothesizing about text currently being read and making predictions about content that is yet to be encountered. However, they note that in practice the two kinds of activities are often intertwined.

Monitoring

Comprehension monitoring enables the reader to become quickly aware of failure to understand the material. Collins and Smith describe four types of failure: failure to understand particular words; failure to understand particular sentences; failure to understand relations between sentences; and failure to understand how the text fits together as a whole.

Failures to understand words form the simplest kind of comprehension problem. They can occur either when the word is new or unfamiliar to the reader, or when the word does not make sense to the reader in the context in which it appears. So far as single sentences are concerned, there are a number of possible reasons for a reader failing to understand. For instance, a person may not be able to think of any interpretation of the sentence that makes sense. Alternatively, the sentence may seem to be ambiguous, and have more than one possible meaning. Another possible reason for a reader failing to understand a sentence is that the content may seem to be too vague to have any clear meaning. A final cause of difficulties is that the meaning of the sentence may seem to conflict with the reader's prior knowledge.

Similarly, there are a number of possible reasons for a person being unable to understand how one sentence relates to another or failing to see how the whole text fits together. A child's guess at the meaning of one sentence may clash with the interpretation of an earlier one. Research by Ellen Markman (1979) and others has shown that children (and older students as well) often fail to detect inconsistencies in text passages. Comprehension failures can also be caused by a child's being unable to see the point of some of the material, or to understand why characters act in the way that is described.

Collins and Smith next discuss some of the remedial actions that readers can take when a comprehension failure occurs. Some of these actions are easy to invoke, without disrupting reading, but others can only be undertaken at the cost of losing the thread of the passage. The first, and least disruptive, of the possible actions is simply to ignore the failure to comprehend, and read on. This may be a sensible thing to do when the failure concerns a word or passage that is not critical for understanding the text as a whole, but in other circumstances ignoring a comprehension failure may have damaging consequences.

Secondly, it may be wise to adopt a 'wait and see' strategy, suspending judgement about how to react to the comprehension failure, in the expectation that the meaning will soon become clearer. Again, in some instances this way of handling the problem will be effective: it certainly avoids disrupting the flow of reading. On other occasions, however, this passive approach will simply lead to difficulties being confounded.

Thirdly, the reader may try to work out what the material means, by making a guess that can be verified or disconfirmed at a later stage. Fourthly, the reader can decide that an even more vigorous response to the failure to understand is necessary, and read again the passage that caused difficulties. Such an action has a definite cost for the reader, however, in that it disrupts the reading process and introduces the risk of losing the thread of the content. Fifthly, if it seems necessary to do so, the reader can take the bigger and inevitably more disruptive step of going back to a previous part of the text. If there is an overload of information, or if there seems to be a contradiction with some material that appeared earlier in the passage, a highly active response such as this may be essential if the meaning of the prose material is to be clarified.

The sixth and final remedial action suggested by Collins and Smith, and the most disruptive of all, is to seek outside help in order to make it clear what something means. The source of help might be a dictionary, or another book, or a person such as a teacher. This kind of action will undoubtedly interrupt the flow of the passage, but it may be the only way to discover the meaning of a word, a sentence, or a larger segment that is crucial for understanding the text as a whole.

Some educators have suggested that too much comprehension monitoring can hinder reading by interfering with it. Collins and Smith disagree. They argue that, on the contrary, continuous monitoring may be necessary on some occasions, if the reader is to gain the full meaning from difficult materials that need to be mastered in detail. They also note, incidentally, that experienced readers may monitor some prose passages automatically, without making any conscious effort to do so. Conceivably, too much monitoring may occasionally cause problems for some readers, but too little monitoring is much more commonly a cause of failures to understand.

Generating and evaluating hypotheses

The activity of making hypotheses about the meaning of a passage, and evaluating them, forms the second of the two components of comprehension which Collins and Smith draw to the attention of teachers. Readers need to make guesses and form tentative hypotheses about the meanings of particular words and sentences, as was mentioned in the previous section. It is equally important for a reader to make more general hypotheses about wider aspects of the text, for instance about the intentions of story characters.

The capable reader makes various kinds of predictions as the text progresses. In order to understand written materials, students need to learn to make hypotheses about future content. Especially with fiction, readers need to use information that enables such predictions to be made. The author may give details about a character that are designed to create expectations in the reader about the character's actions. For example, describing a particular character as having a 'curling lip' provides a clue to his role in a story. The author assumes that the reader will be able to interpret clues concerning (in this case) 'bad guys' and other elements in the text, and will form expectations about their future activities.

Expectations about the general contents of a story are also influenced by information about the situations that characters encounter. A description of a funeral will set up the expectation that people will be sad: the information that a character has gained some kind of success or conquest, or won a prize, creates an expectation of happiness. Giving details about a character's goals or interests is another way of creating expectations. Similarly, providing the information that two characters are in conflict or competition also leads to expectancies on the part of the reader. Particular kinds of genres, such as Westerns, detective stories and romantic fiction, for instance, all have special conventions that produce particular expectations.

Children learn to make predictions as they read a narrative passage. A story would appear very disjointed to a reader who did not make any hypotheses and predictions: these activities hold a story together. Readers rely heavily on their existing knowledge in order to understand a narrative. As we mentioned in chapter 4, children and adults make sense of things by allocating meanings that are plausible in the particular context in which items of information occur. Recall that the reader who encounters 'held up his hand' decides what it means by making an inference on the basis of that part of his existing knowledge to which he is directed by the context. In this case the surrounding parts of the passage provide clues about the author's intended meaning.

If the reader's knowledge includes a highly organized *script* or *schema* about a particular kind of event (going to a theatre or a restaurant, for example) and if the reader has learned that a particular piece of information in the text provides a cue for eliciting such a script, then a story passage may be entirely meaningful even if it excludes most of the information about the detailed activities contained in the script. The author's intention is that the reader will supply for himself the necessary script information. Consequently, a novel might contain, say, a three-page description of two people sharing a meal in a restaurant which mentions hardly any of the events that actually took place, but which is nevertheless entirely understandable. But for this to be possible it is essential that the reader has learned the appropriate comprehension skills. The reader must correctly interpret, consciously or otherwise, the cues in the text that direct him to the appropriate part of his prior knowledge.

Teaching Comprehension Strategies

How are comprehension strategies best taught? What are the most effective ways to teach students to avoid comprehension failures in reading, to remedy them when they do occur, and to utilize cues in the text in order to form good hypotheses and make accurate predictions? Collins and Smith recommend that the teaching should be done in three stages. In the first stage, they suggest, the teacher should demonstrate or *model* the process of comprehending, by providing a kind of running commentary on the comprehension activities that he or she undertakes while reading aloud to a student. The second stage involves students being encouraged to do these things for themselves, and being given guidance whenever necessary, as they read aloud. In the third stage the students practise using their newly gained comprehension skills while they read silently.

Stage One

The activities that the teacher should demonstrate in the modelling stage are ones that we have already described. As the teacher reads aloud, she can generate (aloud) any reasonable hypotheses (for instance, 'He's a bad guy'). Collins and Smith suggest that, up to a point, the more wrong hypotheses that are generated the better. Young students need to learn that hypotheses contribute to comprehension even if they do not turn out to be correct: revising and altering wrong hypotheses is a necessary aspect of comprehension. The teacher should also try to make it clear *why* she is making a particular hypothesis. At a subsequent point in the text, when new evidence that confirms or negates the hypothesis is encountered, the teacher should draw attention to this evidence, indicating its bearing upon the hypothesis. If the new evidence causes the teacher to alter a hypothesis, she should point out why and how it is being changed.

Another comprehension activity to which the teacher can draw students' attention in the modelling stage is noticing items in the text that appear to be incongruous or hard to understand. For example, when she does not understand a word or a sentence, or when she is unsure how two pieces of information are related, she can draw attention to the problem, describing the source of the difficulty and stating how it arises. She can then say aloud how she is attempting to deal with the situation (usually by trying one of the remedial procedures described above). The teacher can also voice aloud any other points that affect understanding of the passage; for instance, insights about the author's intentions, views about the effectiveness of the text, criticisms of the structure or contents, or suggestions about ways in which the text could be made clearer.

In brief, at this stage the teacher is performing aloud the various kinds of activities that contribute to comprehension, which are normally done silently. The purpose is to help students to realize just what kinds of activities are involved in the comprehension aspect of reading, and to see how they are actually performed with a real piece of textual material, and how the various different activities each contribute to making the text understandable.

Stage Two

In the second stage students are encouraged to generate their own hypotheses and perform other comprehension activities for themselves. Collins and Smith suggest that the teacher should start by suggesting possible hypotheses, for instance 'Do you think X will do Y?' Next, the teacher should introduce questions that prompt students to form their own hypotheses, for instance 'What do you think will happen to X?' or 'How do you think the story will end?' Gradually, students begin to generate their own hypotheses spontaneously, without the teacher's constant support.

The teacher can also encourage the students to take an increasingly active role in monitoring comprehension. Instead of the teacher drawing attention to a difficulty, as in the modelling stage, the students themselves begin to do so: they spot comprehension failures and problems and they suggest possible remedies. The authors suggest that students who are given enough encouragement will come to contribute freely to each of the various comprehension activities. In this way, reading becomes a game in which the students all make guesses and predictions and then discover who was right.

Stage Three

In the third stage, where the goal is to have students undertaking comprehension activities independently and silently, the teacher uses various techniques to discover how the students are getting on. For example, in order to assess students' ability to detect sources of difficulty, the teacher may tell them that there is something 'wrong' with the text, and ask them to spot what it is. To assess their choice of remedies, the teacher might give the students prose materials in which problems have been deliberately inserted. She can then discover how the students cope with the difficulties they encounter. Also, inserted questions can be introduced in order to assess a student's skill at making predictions about future text contents while reading silently. With a specially constructed text it is also possible to measure students' competence at forming and testing various different kinds of expectations and hypotheses about future contents.

An Approach to Comprehension Training

The effectiveness of the teaching methods suggested by Collins and Smith has not been formally tested, but some instructional materials that use very similar techniques have been evaluated in an interesting study by Ann Brown, Annemarie Palincsar and Bonnie Armbruster. These authors taught comprehension skills to seventh-grade American children (aged 12 to 13 years) who were, at the outset, very poor at comprehending written materials.

The planning of this research was strongly influenced by the authors' views about the learning of comprehension abilities. One important factor was their belief that situations in which the child has some kind of *dialogue* with an adult, typically the mother, are particularly effective for helping the child to acquire language and to make sense of important aspects of the world. Similar dialogues, involving sequences of close interaction in which the adult helps the child to learn by providing activities that serve to give feedback and to select and focus experiences, are seen by Brown and her colleagues as being central to a child's gaining the capacity to comprehend information that is presented in any of a number of forms, including written text. These authors also believe that in order to help children to learn to understand prose materials the teacher should undertake activities that include making statements aimed at activating relevant existing knowledge and questioning students' basic assumptions, in addition to using the specific teaching devices that are proposed by Collins and Smith. Brown and her colleagues list a number of activities that help readers understand written materials. These are:

1 Making the purposes of reading clear, and understanding the explicit and implicit demands of the task.
2 Activating relevant information from the reader's existing knowledge.
3 Directing attention effectively in order to focus concentration on the major content rather than less important details.
4 Evaluating content for internal consistency and compatibility with prior knowledge and common sense.
5 Monitoring ongoing activities in order to check that the text is being understood, by engaging in activities such as self-testing and periodically reviewing the content.
6 Drawing and testing kinds of inferences, including interpretations, predictions and conclusions.

Some of these skills overlap with one another to a large extent. For example, Item 2, activating prior knowledge (an activity which, as was emphasized in chapter 4, is crucial to learning and understanding in many different circumstances, not only in connection with comprehension) and Item 4, evaluating content for internal consistency and compatibility with existing knowledge, involve very similar skills. Of the six items listed by these authors, Items 4, 5 and 6 are virtually identical to ones emphasized by Collins and Smith.

The training studies

Brown and her colleagues decided to concentrate on training four particular skills: *summarizing, questioning, clarifying* and *predicting*. Note that each of these skills can be regarded as an important element of learning how to learn. Each of them is discussed as a separate skill at some point in the present book, either in this chapter or elsewhere. In the case of most of the skills, a substantial amount of research has been undertaken in order to investigate their importance and to develop and evaluate effective training programmes.

A crucial aspect of these instructional programmes is that all the different component activities are taught and are utilized *together*. The authors point out that whilst we know a great deal about the use of these activities in isolation we know very little about 'the spontaneous orchestration of a battery of such activities' in order to deal with comprehension failures.

In the present series of training studies each of the above skills was utilized in order to respond to concrete problems encountered in comprehending actual text materials. Summarizing was carried out in order to report what had already been described in the text and to test for understanding. Clarifying occurred when a reader was confused about the meaning of a passage. Questioning was used as a concrete task, and it was always tied to a part of the text.

In accordance with the authors' views about the value of instructional dialogues, the training procedure was also designed to incorporate certain aspects of a dialogue between mother and child. There was considerable interaction between student and teacher, and much reciprocal questioning, paraphrasing, clarifying and predicting. There were three training studies in all. In the first two of them an investigator worked with the children, individually or in pairs. The third study was conducted by regular teachers in the school classroom.

Study One. The first study began with a number of assessment procedures, designed to measure as accurately as possible the students' initial comprehension skills and their weaknesses before the training started. The actual training period lasted for about three weeks. Six months later the students were tested again, and they afterwards received some further training. Four students participated as subjects in the study.

During the training period, a typical procedure involved the investigator and a student engaging together at an interactive learning game in which each of them took turns to lead a dialogue concerning the text passage they were reading. Thus both the investigator and the student took turns to 'teach' the successive paragraphs. With a new passage, the investigator might start by drawing attention to the title, and asking the student to make predictions about the contents and think about the possible relationship of the passage to the student's existing knowledge. Next, the student and the investigator silently read the first paragraph. Then the partner whose turn it was to 'teach' that segment would summarize it aloud, discuss and clarify any difficulties, invent a test question about the passage, of the kind that a teacher might ask, and, finally, make a prediction about the content of the remainder of the text.

The investigator would try to ensure that all these events were embedded in a reasonably natural dialogue, with each partner giving feedback to the other. The students were carefully told *why* each of the activities was useful. They were shown how all the different mental activities contributed to the ability to understand written materials.

The students did not find it at all easy at first to take their part in the dialogue. The adult had to give them a good deal of help, based on prompting techniques, praise and encouragement, and detailed feedback. In the earliest sessions the students were relatively passive, and the investigator spent much of the time modelling effective strategies. As the sessions progressed, however, the students became increasingly expert at leading the dialogue. Here are some examples of the remarks and comments that were contributed by the investigator:

> If you're having a hard time summarizing, why don't you think of a question first?
>
> You asked that question well; it was very clear what information you wanted.
>
> A question I would have asked would be. . . .

The training was extremely successful. Findings obtained from a number of objective measures showed that the procedures were highly effective. For example, in the first sessions 46 per cent of the questions produced by the students were either judged not to be proper questions or needed clarification, but by the final sessions only 2 per cent of the responses were in this category. Similarly, the percentage of students' summaries that were judged to have captured the main ideas rose from 11 per cent to 60 per cent. By the later sessions the students' questions were similar to those constructed by the teacher, and used the questioner's own words rather than just repeating words in the textual passage.

To provide an independent measure of the effectiveness of the comprehension skills the students were also questioned about prose passages which they read on their own, outside the training sessions. At the beginning, their success rate averaged only 15 per cent. This rose to over 80 per cent during the training sessions. When the students were tested six months later the number of correct answers averaged 60 per cent, and their rate of success rose again to over 80 per cent after just one day of renewed training.

The students were also given a social studies comprehension test in their own classroom, administered by the classroom teacher, in order to assess the generalization of their newly acquired comprehension skills to the classroom setting. At the beginning of the study, their scores had placed them in the bottom 15 per cent of seventh-grade students, for comprehension skills. By the end of the training, however, each student rose to a higher percentile rank. The increases for the four students were respectively 20 per cent (i.e. moving from the fifteenth percentile of students of that age to the thirty-fifth percentile), 46 per cent, 4 per cent and 34 per cent.

In summary, the findings of a number of separate tests, in the students' regular classroom as well as in the training environment, all demonstrated substantial improvements in comprehension. The training was very successful.

Studies two and three. The second study was similar in most respects but it also included a number of tests that were designed to measure transfer of the trained skills to comprehension activities such as detecting errors in texts and rating the relative importance of different parts of a narrative. Again, the training was highly successful. Of the six students in the second study, none of whom averaged more than 40 per cent on comprehension tests administered before the training session, within 15 days of training all but one achieved a stable level of 75 per cent or more on five successive days. In five students out of six there was substantial generalization of skills to the classroom environment. They had an average improvement of 37 percentile points in their ranking in the classroom, in relation to other students in the same grade. On three of the four transfer tests that were administered the students demonstrated significant improvements.

In the third and final study it was decided to provide the instruction in the realistic naturally occurring circumstances of a regular school classroom, with classroom teachers giving the training. The study was preceded by three sessions in which the teachers were carefully taught to follow the procedures used in the earlier studies. Then the teachers taught their students, in four groups ranging in numbers from four to seven.

The results of the third study were very similar to the earlier findings. There were large and reliable improvements in comprehension, according to each of a number of separate measures. The small decline in comprehension scores that occurred after a six-month period was rapidly remedied, in one training session. The training also transferred successfully to comprehension skills other than those that were taught.

Some conclusions

The authors consider some of the possible reasons for the success of their training procedures, in contrast to other training studies that have failed to produce durable improvements or ones that transfer to other tasks. First, they point out, the training was extensive: it involved a considerable amount of time and effort. Secondly, the particular skills that were taught were ones that had been carefully specified in the context of a theoretical account of comprehension processes. A lack of such skills was known to cause problems for poor readers. Third, the training was tailored to the needs of the particular students. These individuals were able to carry out the decoding skills required for reading but they lacked the active skills necessary for effective comprehension. Fourth, the skills chosen were ones that could be expected to be useful in a variety of different learning situations. Also, emphasis was placed on making sure that students fully understood the importance of the skills and activities they learned in the training sessions. Finally, the interactive dialogue context provided a number of useful advantages over alternative ways of teaching.

The research that has been described in the present chapter demonstrates that carefully designed training that is based on a knowledge of the skills that underlie the ability to learn from the written word can produce large and genuine improvements. It is not at all easy to bring about substantial increases in comprehension, but the research of Ann Brown and her colleagues shows that it can be done.

In other chapters we have described numerous findings demonstrating that it is possible to improve students' performance at many of the sub-skills that are needed for classroom learning tasks. An especially valuable feature of the present series of studies is that they show that it is also possible to devise training procedures in which such such skills are taught together in a co-ordinated fashion, resulting in striking practical gains in the ability to understand written materials.

8

Writing Skills

The previous chapter described ways to help students learn *from* written materials. In the present chapter we shall consider techniques that contribute to the ability to *produce* information in written form. The production of prose descriptions by a student requires most of the skills necessary for understanding texts, but it also demands other abilities, and it is more difficult.

From Conversation to Written Communication

Most children are reasonably effective at giving descriptions in *spoken* language. Written communication draws upon many of the language abilities we use in talking to other people. But communicating in writing is much harder, largely because the writer has to manage without the many verbal and non-verbal aids to communication that people can depend on when they talk to each other. For example, in a conversation each partner can help the other in a variety of ways. They can signal to the other person when to proceed, when to stop, when repetition of a point or further explanation is required, when to move to another topic, and indicate when full understanding depends upon additional information being provided (Bereiter and Scardamalia, 1982). The listener's need for additional information may be communicated through body language – a puzzled stare, a nod of the head – or through words, for instance in a question such as 'But how did you get there in the first place?'

With written communication none of these aids is present. The writer has to be completely explicit and must plan the composition carefully in order to include all the necessary information. Many people never gain the ability to express themselves clearly in writing. Amongst all the achievements that school learning promotes, written communication is arguably both the most valuable and the hardest to learn.

The young writer has to learn to combine a number of different skills. In the present chapter we examine two learned achievements, note-taking and making summaries, that make use of skills which students can also draw upon for lengthier written communications. We also consider ways in which students can be helped to acquire other abilities that can play a direct part in the process of composing written texts.

Note-Taking

The most obviously useful outcome of taking notes is to provide oneself with a convenient record of needed information. (However, the information that appears in students' notes is often surprisingly inaccurate, as Hartley and Cameron, 1967, observed.) But there are other possible effects that have implications for students' progress at learning how to learn.

First, the note-taking activities that take place when a student is either listening to the teacher or reading a text passage may help the learner attend to the material being studied. It is by no means always easy to give sustained attention to information to be learned, especially when it is difficult: any activity that can make it easier for a student to attend may prove beneficial. There are wide variations between students in the amount of time they spend actively engaged on school tasks. Attention, as measured by a student's 'time on task', as distinct from 'time available' for learning, is positively correlated with school achievement (Bloom, 1974; Glaser, 1982). Secondly, it is possible that a student who, as a result of taking notes, provides himself or herself with a form of the material that is in that individual's own words thereby acquires a version of the information that is especially clear or meaningful. Thirdly, the actual processing and coding *activities* that occur when a student takes notes may have direct effects upon learning. Evidence described in chapter 2 demonstrated that those kinds of input processing of perceived information that involve careful attention to its meaning have a strongly positive influence upon remembering.

Investigating the effects of taking notes

In practice, it is not easy to disentangle the evidence concerning these three possible effects of note-taking, but it is clear that the activity does influence learning, and has outcomes other than that of recording needed information. One experiment by the author (Howe, 1970) was designed to investigate in some detail the relationship between individual students' note-taking activities and subsequent learning. Students were asked to listen to a prose passage and take notes on it. They were told to keep the notes brief but to try to retain the important elements in the passage. Immediately afterwards they gave their notes to the experimenter (and they were unable to use the notes later for revision purposes). One week afterwards there was a recall test, in which the students were asked to write down whatever they could remember of the content of the original passage.

When the students' attempts at recall were scored, it was found that, on average, they remembered around four of the twenty meaningful parts of the passage. The experimenter was especially interested in discovering the relationship between the detailed *content* of each student's attempt at recall and the content of the same person's notes. Inspection of the notes revealed that the average number of the 20 meaningful elements from the text that appeared in an individual's notes was 10.8. The question of particular interest was, what is the relationship between an item from the passage being recorded in a person's notes and that same person remembering the item?

For each individual student, considering only those items which that person had recorded in his or her notes, the probability of such an item also being recalled in the test administered a week afterwards was, on average, one in three. However, the probability of an item that did *not* appear in an individual's notes being recalled was very much lower, only one in twenty. In other words, the likelihood of a particular item being recalled was very strongly influenced by whether that same item had been recorded in the student's notes, despite the fact that, since the notes were taken away from the students immediately after they had been made, there was no opportunity to consult them before the recall test.

There are a number of possible reasons for the contents of students' notes and the same individuals' recall attempts being so closely related. It is possible, for instance, that taking notes on some elements of the passage makes it difficult for the listener to attend to other parts. Also, the particular items that appear in a student's notes may partly reflect that individual's judgement about the relative importance of the different parts of the text, and the same judgements may also affect recall. In any case, despite any uncertainties concerning the detailed explanation of the findings, it is clear that attentional processes are involved: the particular ways in which individuals direct their note-taking activities have powerful effects in determining what is actually learned.

Effects of repeated recall attempts

The above note-taking study provides a down-to-earth demonstration of a principle discussed in chapter 2, that what students actively *do* and what they *learn* are closely connected. However, combining this observation with the known tendency for previous knowledge to influence remembering of new events, sometimes adversely (see chapter 4) suggests the possibility that mistaken versions of events that are produced by inaccurate note-taking or related activities may be hard to eradicate. Such a possibility was examined in a further experiment.

Students listened to a passage taken from a novel, and afterwards they tried to recall the information. An unusual feature about the experiment was that the students listened to the passage and tried to recall it on several separate occasions. Following their attempt to remember the passage they listened to it again, and a week later they were asked to try again to recall it. Again, afterwards the passage was presented once more. A week after that, the students again attempted recall, and once again they listened to the original passage. In all, there were four presentations of the same passage, and the students made four separate attempts to recall it.

The findings concerning overall accuracy of remembering in the successive sessions did not yield any great surprises. The most striking aspect of these results was the rather small increase in accuracy of remembering from week to week: recall rose from around eight out of twenty meaningful segments in the first test to around twelve out of twenty in the final test.

Much more remarkable, however, were the findings that emerged from an examination of the detailed contents of individuals' successive attempts to recall the passage from one week to the next. On each of these occasions, the actual information that each particular student remembered from the passage was extremely similar. That is to say, the students were extremely good at remembering exactly what they had recalled on the previous recall tests (and at remembering any errors that they had introduced on previous occasions) and extremely bad at either remembering information from the passage which they had *not* previously recalled or correcting previous errors. This is despite the fact that the correct version of the passage was presented on four separate occasions, and on each occasion the students were visibly interested in spotting their mistakes and trying to ensure that they would now retain the correct version of the passage.

Despite all the students' efforts, they seemed to learn much less from the repetitions of the correct versions than from their own activity in trying to remember the information. For instance, if a meaningful item was recalled on each of the first three attempts, the probability of it being recalled correctly again on the fourth trial was .98, but the probability of an item that was not recalled on the first three tests being remembered on the fourth was only .2, despite the fact that subjects had by that stage listened to the original passage on no less than four occasions. Note also that these probabilities refer to the number of *meaningful ideas* remembered, and not to the literal recall of particular words.

A Classroom Implication. This finding has a definite implication for classroom teaching, apart from giving a further demonstration that what students learn largely depends upon what they do. It is not uncommon for teachers to give students a test and later 'go over' the correct answers, on the assumption that after students have been told the correct answers to the questions they will subsequently remember them. The present findings indicate that such an assumption is ill-founded, and that students are much more likely to go on remembering their own wrong answers to test questions. As Robert Glaser (1982) has noted, we need to be cautious about accepting the general notion that 'practice makes perfect', since it is quite common for children to practise errors and misconceptions and to practise in ways that do not lead to useful learning.

Simply being told the right answer to a question is not enough to ensure that it will be retained. What is required is some procedure whereby the student is able to arrive at the correct answer for himself, even if this necessitates a fair amount of effort and retracing of earlier steps.

Precisely how this is best achieved will depend on the particular circumstances, but it is important that the mental processing involved (or 'mental effort') is at least as extensive as the mental activity that originally led to the student remembering an incorrect version of the information.

Note-taking style and student learning

To return to note-taking as such, the author's research (Howe, 1970) has also shown that what a student note-taker actually learns from the material on which the notes are made may be related to the manner in which notes are produced. In the note-taking study described earlier, the investigator counted the number of words that appeared in each student's notes, and he also counted the number of meaningful ideas from the passage that were successfully communicated in those notes. Dividing the number of *ideas* successfully recorded by the number of *words* that an individual student needed to record them provides a ratio which might be regarded as being an indication of the *efficiency* of that student's note-taking: it is a measure of the extent to which that student was successful in communicating a large amount of meaningful content in few words. At the same time it provides a rough indication of the extent to which the student transformed the original passage into his or her own words.

The question is, does a relationship exist between the ratios obtained in this way and students' actual learning, as measured by scores on the test of recall administered a week after the information was originally presented to the students, at which time they made their notes? The answer is 'Yes': there was a positive correlation (+.53) between individual students' ratios (obtained by dividing the number of ideas in their notes by the number of words) and their recall of the information in the prose passage.

This finding does not by itself prove that individual differences in note-taking practices cause differences in learning. The correlation between the two measures is equally likely to have been due to the fact that the mental activities necessary for taking 'efficient' notes are ones that also lead to accurate retention. Nevertheless, it is useful to have our attention drawn to the fact that measures of the outcomes of note-taking activities (in common with various other kinds of activities, as we have seen) and measures of how much students learn are definitely related to each other. Note also that in normal classroom circumstances, any differences in the effectiveness for learning of note-taking *activities* are compounded by differences in the value of the notes that are actually produced. Pupils typically make extensive use of their own notes, for revision and other purposes. At this stage it is undoubtedly useful to have 'good' notes, in which the required information is effectively recorded.

Using pre-prepared notes

Some teachers dictate notes to their students or provide them with notes that the teacher has prepared. Doing so can be a convenient way of enabling students to have a written version of required information, but it is done at the cost of depriving students of the value of making notes for themselves. In some situations the added convenience of pre-prepared notes may compensate for this.

In certain instances it may be sensible to encourage students to take notes for themselves but to provide extra notes at a later stage for those individuals who need them. In one study (Howe and Godfrey, 1977) British students at a sixth-form college were asked to listen to and take notes on a somewhat rambling and unorganized historical passage describing an early Chinese dynasty. Afterwards they were tested for recall of the passage contents. Then some of the students were told to revise from their own notes, and the other students were provided with a version of the information that was much more clearly organized than the passage of text they had listened to. Later, all the students were tested again for long-term retention of the information.

The most interesting finding was that giving students the organized written version of the text helped some students considerably, but others did not benefit at all. Those students who performed relatively well in the original test did not benefit from being provided with the highly organized version that had been prepared for them. That is to say, for those students whose original test scores were in the top quarter, subsequent test performance was no better if they were given the organized version than if they had to revise from the notes they had made for themselves. However, for students who did badly in the original recall test, giving them the organized version of the material brought considerable advantages. These students (whose initial test scores were in the bottom quarter), subsequently performed much better if they were able to use the organized version than if they had to rely on their own notes.

Clearly, the procedure of giving students the highly organized written version of the material to be learned was a very helpful one for some but not at all useful for others. This finding serves as a useful reminder that in most school learning situations the value of a particular method or procedure greatly depends upon its appropriateness for the particular learners who use it. A procedure that is extremely useful for some learners may be much less so for others.

Learning to Take Notes

Like any other skill, note-taking needs to be learned. All too often it is assumed that by the time students reach a certain age they have somehow gained the ability to make notes without ever having received instruction in how to do so.

The note-taker has to record important items of information without wasting time and effort in writing down non-essential items. For the child who is beginning to learn to take notes two kinds of preparatory activities can be particularly useful. The first is simply to underline the important words in a passage that the child is reading. This provides needed practice that helps a learner to gain expertise in detecting which are the most important words in a passage of text. The kind of 'dialogue' learning situation that was described in chapter 7, in connection with comprehension skills, can be particularly effective for helping children to identify the important parts of a text passage. For example, teacher and child can take turns in going through a passage and underlining the important words, at the same time saying *why* they are important. There is some evidence that simply underlining important items can have a positive effect on learning prose materials: it was found in one study that underlining improved students' learning of information from a 6000 word text passage.

A similar but slightly more difficult preparatory exercise for children who are beginning to learn how to take notes involves writing down the most important words. For instance, a child might be asked to write down the three most important words in each sentence. Again, it is also useful to ask the children to say why they think that particular words are especially important, and to help them to acquire the sub-skill of detecting those words that are most crucial. Like underlining, writing down important words can itself aid learning. In one study (Howe and Godfrey, 1977) we found that students who were told to record the three words that they considered most important in each sentence of a prose passage recalled the passage as accurately as students who tried to write down the entire text. Those students who were successful in choosing crucial words recalled more items than students whose word choices were less appropriate.

Making Summaries

The ability to make summaries draws upon similar skills to those involved in note-taking. Summarizing is often valuable, and being able to do so is essential for students who need to produce written reports, compositions and essays. But as with note-taking, whilst the value of summarizing is widely acknowledged, children are not often given systematic instruction aimed at helping them to make summaries of texts.

Jeanne Day has listed five simple rules for students to follow in making summaries (Brown and Day, 1983), as follows:

1   Delete unimportant information. A summary should not contain information that is trivial.
2   Delete redundant information. Summaries should not be repetitive.
3   Use subordinates in place of lists of items.
4   If possible 'lift' from the passage a topic sentence stating the main theme, and put it in the summary.
5   If there is no topic sentence, make one up for the summary.

Setting out definite rules to follow is often helpful for young students. By the age of 12 most children can use the first three of the above rules, with little or no instruction. The others are more difficult, but training was effective in improving students' performance at making summaries. Day taught summarizing skills to students of varying ability. For all of them, Rules 4 and 5 were the most difficult to put into practice, but all except the least capable of the students were eventually able to follow all five rules.

Learning Skills for Writing

In learning how to write effectively it is necessary to combine and co-ordinate an intimidating variety of skills. So many different skills are involved, most of them dependent on each other, that writing may seem for the beginner to be an impossible task. As one leading researcher into children's writing, Marlene Scardamalia, remarks,

> To pay conscious attention to handwriting, spelling, punctuation, word choice, syntax, textual connections, purpose, organization, clarity, rhythm, euphony, and reader characteristics would seemingly overload the information processing capacity of the best intellects. For the skilled writer we may suppose that many aspects of writing are automated and that cognitive space-saving strategies make writing possible without inordinate demands on processing capacity. For the beginning writer, however, very little is automated and coping strategies are lacking. (Scardamalia, 1981, p. 81)

Nevertheless, Scardamalia observes, most children do learn to write, and some even enjoy it. The necessary abilities are not acquired quickly or easily, but over a period of years children gradually become increasingly successful at expressing their thoughts in writing.

Writing problems and remedial activities

At the beginning of the chapter we mentioned some of the demands of writing that are not encountered in spoken language, as in a conversation. Some of the particular problems that a child encounters in progressing from conversation to written conversation have been summarized by Scardamalia and one of her colleagues (Bereiter and Scardamalia, 1982), together with suitable intervention activities by which teachers can help to overcome the problems.

Inadequate quantity of text. First, there are a number of problems that a child meets when learning to generate text in the absence of a conversational partner or respondent. For example, the quantity of text that a young child may produce may be limited to the length of a single turn in a conversation, which is clearly insufficient for writing purposes. In this event, the suggestion is that a teacher should merely prompt the child to 'say more'. Simple interventions of this kind can lead to large increases in the quantity of text produced, with no deterioration of quality. Another suggested procedure is to ask the child to produce a kind of 'slow dictation'. This involves producing language orally, without the mechanical burden of having to write things down. Again, such interventions have proved successful in helping children to produce prose passages that are considerably longer than is usual in face-to-face conversation.

Knowing what to write. Secondly, children can have problems in knowing what to write, even when they are prompted to produce more. They need help in order to learn how to search their own memories for suitable content. Bereiter and Scardamalia have had success with a number of procedures for helping children to overcome this source of difficulty. One device is to give prompts that provide 'openers' for sentences, but stopping short of cueing specific information. For example, they tried giving children a set of openers such as 'I think . . .', 'for example . . .', and 'Even though. . .'. They discovered that many children aged between nine and fourteen can use these openers to increase their written output.

Planning. A third kind of problem encountered in going from conversational to written expression is that much more planning is necessary. In young children, planning may be limited to decisions about 'What shall I say next?', and this may be decided by writing down anything that comes to mind which is related to the topic. Thus,

> A common composition tactic of young writers is to tell all they know on a topic irrespective of the writing assignment. For example, when writing an essay on winter, the child might begin with 'I think winter is the best time of year because you can make snowmen'; the child will then proceed for many more sentences telling all she knows about snowmen. Having exhausted that topic, the child will declare that

the composition is ended, seemingly having 'forgotten' the original purpose of the essay. (Brown and Day, 1983, p. 13)

Children's planning tends to lack the 'attention to the whole' that is found in mature people's written compositions. They frequently proceed one step at a time without much organization in advance.

Bereiter and Scardamalia used a number of techniques for helping children learn to make plans. One involved giving children final sentences, and telling them to build their compositions towards those endings. For example, in one training session 12-year-olds had to make up a story that ended with the sentence, 'And so, after considering the reasons for it and the reasons against it, the duke decided to rent his castle to the vampire after all, in spite of the rumour he had heard.'

Given this task, the children worked together on a plan for the story. The children did not find it at all easy, but they soon realized that it was necessary to think of reasons for and against the decision to rent the castle, and they eventually made progress towards finding a solution that made a good story. Discussing the planning problems in a group provides useful opportunities for children to learn to achieve the kinds of planning that a writer must eventually do alone.

9

Motivation and Learning

Introduction

If a competition were to take place to decide on the person in recent history whose achievements at learning have been the most stunning, my vote would go to a nineteenth-century Englishman, Sir Richard Burton. It would be wrong to claim that his contributions to mankind are on a par with those of a Darwin or an Einstein, both of whom chose to concentrate their energies in particular directions, thereby maximizing the impact of their work. But Burton's achievements were on a broader front. He excelled at practically everything.

A list of Burton's feats gives at least a faint indication of the man's prodigious powers. He is best known for his translation into English of sixteen volumes of the stories known as the *Arabian Nights*. He also translated large quantities of Portugese literature, folklore of many countries and Latin poetry. His own poems were published in two volumes. He wrote two authoritative books on swords and swordsmanship. In an age of Victorian heroes, he was outstanding as an explorer and traveller. He journeyed in search of the origins of the Nile, and he made numerous dangerous expeditions of discovery in northern Africa and the Near East. One of his journeys took him to the sacred city of Mecca, sternly forbidden to non-Muslims and penetrated by only a handful of Europeans before Burton. His account makes compelling reading, and it is clear that he needed breathtaking powers of tenacity, courage and sheer cunning in order to build and maintain a false identity as a man of the East, in addition to undergoing the rigours of an arduous and lengthy journey.

As well as being an adventurer and explorer, Burton was a profound scholar, avid for knowledge of the countries he visited and the cultures and customs of their peoples. He wrote well over thirty books about his explorations and studies, and he played a large part in establishing the science of anthropology.

Perhaps the most impressive of all Burton's accomplishments in learning was his mastery, to a high level of proficiency, of no less than forty separate languages, plus a substantial number of related dialects. Forty languages! Mastering *four* languages would be an impressive feat by most people's standards, and five or six is outstanding, but acquiring forty languages, *and* all of Burton's many other remarkable achievements, puts Burton into a class beyond superlatives. A genuine Superman!

Is there any key that can help account for Burton's amazing achievements as a learner? I think *motivation* provides such a key, at least to his success at mastering foreign languages.

A glance at his early life does not at first reveal any obvious clues. His forebears were not intellectually exceptional: genetic factors do not appear to have unduly favoured Burton. Nor does his early environment appear to have been appreciably richer or more stimulating than was usual for children from his class and background. His parents took reasonable care to provide their children with competent tutors, but their doing so was not exceptional.

Burton did not hit upon any particular method or technique for language learning that might have made the task especially easy for him, or given him a special advantage. He has left an interesting account of the methods and study habits he followed when he was learning a new language, and there seems to have been nothing extraordinary about his techniques for studying. Undoubtedly he was very systematic in his approach to learning unfamiliar languages and he went about the task with extraordinary persistence. But he reported that he did not find acquiring foreign languages at all easy, and he wrote with feeling about the difficult and time-consuming nature of the learning tasks he set for himself.

What did set Burton apart as a learner were his remarkable powers of energy, determination and sheer doggedness. To learn a new language, Burton would set aside long periods of time for study and he refused to be deflected. He worked and worked, and he kept at the task, persevering in the face of all the discouragement, boredom, frustration and fatigue that can wear down even the most enthusiastic and determined student.

The young Richard Burton was a bright lad, although no infant prodigy, and despite the fact that his early life reveals few hints of future intellectual excellence, it is in his childhood that a key is to be found to the dogged determination which made his efforts to learn so persistent, and eventually so successful. An unusual feature of his childhood years is that they were mostly spent abroad. His father being a gentleman of limited income and no remunerative profession, it was financially advantageous for the family to spend much of their time away from Britain, in various parts of continental Europe. Therefore, if the high-spirited Burton children were to play with others of their own age, they had to acquire the necessary language skills. So the energetic and outgoing young Richard Burton was repeatedly placed in a position in which the effort of learning a new language was amply justified and quickly rewarded.

By the time he reached adolescence he had gained considerable language skills, in addition to a good deal of general experience in acquiring new languages, and also the confidence that came from knowing that this was something at which he could succeed. By adulthood, language-acquisition tasks that to others might have appeared dauntingly large, excruciatingly tedious, of questionable value, and with slim chances of eventual mastery, would have looked very different to the young Burton. He knew that he could succeed because he had done it before: he knew that the effort was justified, because he had reaped the rewards of his own efforts in the past. Undoubtedly the task was difficult, and persisting at it was an enormous strain, but Burton could draw strength and courage from the firm conviction that his persistence would be amply repaid.

Getting Hooked on Learning: The Example of Video Games

Children and older people often get 'hooked' on activities that appear to others to be just as difficult and time-consuming as those that form the main tasks of the classroom learner. In Sir Richard Burton's case, it would not be absurd to say that he was hooked on learning languages, or even 'addicted' to that arduous pursuit. There are many instances of children who seem happy to dedicate large parts of their life to such activities as ballet, acting, sports and music, and they sometimes succeed in gaining outstanding achievements. Undoubtedly there are dangers involved in too much concentration on one aspect of life, especially when it is at the expense of other experiences, but there is no harm in enquiring whether there are things that teachers can do to encourage pupils to get hooked on school learning.

Consider the current interest in video games. Why video games? Because learning at school and playing video games are in certain ways remarkably similar. On the one hand certain video games are remarkably successful at attracting the sustained and concentrated attention of young people, who find them intriguing, compelling and even addictive. On the other hand video games share many of the characteristics of school learning activities: they require close attention and concentration over lengthy periods of time; they demand careful planning and good decision-making; and they necessitate concentration on details whilst distractions are carefully ignored. If we can discover why people, and children especially, become hooked on video games, perhaps this knowledge can be used to help students to become more highly motivated to learn while they are at school.

In a book called *Mind at Play: The Psychology of Video Games* the authors, Geoffrey and Elizabeth Loftus (1983), set out to explain why people find the games so compelling. As a fairly typical example of a game they describe *Pac-Man*, in which a little yellow creature, whose movements are controlled by the player, glides around a complex maze and gobbles up the yellow dots that it contains. However, as he does so he is pursued by four monsters, each in a different colour, which eat Pac-Man if they catch him. There are various ways for Pac-Man to outwit the monsters and escape from them. One means is simply to avoid them. Another is to eat an *energizer*, which is a glowing dot, situated at one of the corners of the video screen. The result of Pac-Man's eating an energizer is to turn some or all of the monsters blue, and whilst a monster remains blue any contact between it and Pac-Man results in the destruction of the monster, not Pac-Man. But after a short time the monsters return to their usual colour; and even if Pac-Man succeeds in destroying a monster it does not stay destroyed for long: it returns to action after a brief spell in the penalty box.

Despite the monsters, Pac-Man may succeed in eating all the dots in the maze. If this happens, a 'new board' appears, with a fresh set of dots. But with each new board things get more difficult. The monsters move faster, Pac-Man moves slower, and when Pac-Man's eating the energizer renders the monsters blue and impotent they remain so for shorter periods of time.

What makes Pac-Man so absorbing? An important factor is that the player is *rewarded* in various ways. For instance, gobbling up the dots gains points for the player, and so does destroying the monsters. In the middle of the board there is a symbol, which indicates how many boards the player has mastered. There is a cherry on the first board, a strawberry on the second board, and on the twelfth board a key appears. The symbols that indicate that a large number of boards have been accomplished bring prestige to the player, and Pac-Man can gain further points by eating the actual symbols.

The above account is a simplified one. There are other rewarding events for the player, such as amusing screen activities between boards. Most importantly, the number of points that a player can earn rapidly increases as expertise is gained. A beginner might get a score of 1000, rising to, say, 5000 after a few games. But such a player will be tantalized to discover that experts can score 50,000 or 100,000 or even more!

Reinforcement

Loftus and Loftus show that the compelling nature of Pac-Man and other video games is best explained by referring to the psychological concept of *reinforcement*. This concept has a central role in most of the theories of animal learning and behaviour that were developed in the early part of the twentieth century. In humans, reinforcers affect learning, but they do so indirectly, through influencing a person's *behaviour*.

A reinforcer is defined quite simply by B. F. Skinner (1938) as being an event that raises the probability of a behaviour which it follows. For example, if giving a rat food every time it turns to the right increases the frequency of the rat's turning right, food is said to be a reinforcer for that response. For our purposes, it is important to know that the *scheduling* of reinforcing events has large effects on an animal's behaviour. Scheduling refers to factors such as the frequency and timing of reinforcers, and the proportion of appropriate behaviours that are reinforced. It might appear that a reinforcer has the strongest effects on behaviour when every appropriate action is reinforced, but in fact that is far from being the case (Howe, 1980). As it happens, behaviours are most likely to be maintained (in technical terms, resistant to *extinction*) when only a relatively small proportion of reponses are reinforced, and when there is a degree of randomness in the frequency and timing of the reinforcing events, so that the animal never knows exactly when it will be reinforced.

It is suggested by Geoffrey and Elizabeth Loftus that much of the compelling nature of Pac-Man and similar games lies in their incorporating highly effective schedules of reinforcement. In video games, some but by no means all players' actions are reinforced, the frequency of rewards being variable and unpredictable, a combination of circumstances which produces considerable resistance to extinction. Occasional and irregular rewards contribute to video games being irrestibly compelling, just as they produce high and sustained levels of responding in the rat. One feature that sets video games apart from games that are not based on computers is that the former can be programmed to be easy at first and then get progressively more difficult, so that an optimal schedule of reinforcement is maintained as the player's skill increases.

There are other aspects of reinforcement that can be manipulated in video games to exert the maximum effects on the player's behaviour, and further increase the games' addictive qualities. For example, *delays* in reinforcing are usually eliminated. This factor is important: short delays usually lead to reinforcement effects being largest. Also, the *magnitude* of reinforcers can be carefully controlled. Larger rewards lead to faster responding and greater resistance to extinction, even when the rewards are symbolic, in the form of points. (When numbers get too high they all mean very much the same thing for most people, so ten pounds seems much more rewarding than one pound, but ten million pounds is not greatly more attractive than one million pounds. Good games designers make astute use of knowledge of this kind.) Thirdly, there are a number of different ways in which a player can be reinforced. In Pac-Man, for instance, the player can eat dots, avoid monsters, eat energizers, eat symbols, get through boards, gain points, watch amusing activities between boards, and hear music played. This adds to the variety of potential reinforcers, and helps produce a game that will appeal to a variety of people who enjoy different things.

Reinforcers in the classroom. It would be silly to suggest that the important factors in school learning can or should be reduced to the elements of successful video games. However, illustrating the important contribution of carefully scheduled reinforcers towards making these games as compelling as they are should at least alert us to the motivational importance of giving the school learner sufficient rewards, support and encouragement for making progress in the classroom.

As we have seen, school learning typically depends upon individual learners undertaking appropriate strategies and other activities. Often, the nature of the learning task will ensure that these activities are reinforced, but it cannot be taken for granted that this will happen. Classroom reinforcers that incorporated some of the ingenuity that video-games inventors have applied might produce some major gains in classroom motivation.

Motivation and Success at School

The importance of motivation for school success cannot be exaggerated. However, the manner in which motivational factors influence learning is not always straightforward. It is not just a matter of a child wishing to achieve an eventual goal: if that were the case it might be hard to account for the many thousands of youngsters who wish to become brain surgeons or veterinarians but fail to do so. In the case of Sir Richard Burton, for instance, is clear that in addition to having the desire to learn new languages he gained at an early age both a considerable amount of what we might call 'know-how' and, equally important, confidence in his ability to succeed. Such confidence comes from past success yielding rewards for one's efforts and encouragement to believe that eventual goals are really attainable.

However strong the average ten-year-old's desire to become, say, a brain surgeon, in the absence of appropriate rewards and encouragement throughout the lengthy period between the initial wish to succeed and the eventual far-off attainment of success, the chances of such success are extremely slim.

The many aims, intentions, wants, drives, wishes, hopes and desires that comprise the motivational forces in a student's life do not all work in the same direction. Moreover, many of the motives that guide students' classroom behaviour are largely outside the teacher's control. For example, the desire for approval of his or her peers has distracted many a child from working hard at school tasks.

The chances of success at those achievements that demand sustained effort throughout years of schooling are highest when a student can draw upon constant support and encouragement from her family. The value of long-term effort and planning for the future is most readily apparent to a child who can see at first-hand, perhaps in a brother or a sister, the rewards that come from persisting at arduous learning tasks.

Family effects

A hierarchy of needs?

Different needs are more or less important at different times. The *hierarchical need system* of Abraham Maslow illustrates the fact that some basic needs predominate over other motives, and that various wants and desires become more prominent as other needs are filled. According to Maslow, individuals act to satisfy basic physiological needs and the need for safety, and only when these are satisfied do other needs, for instance for love and belonging and for self-esteem, become important. The need to know and understand predominates, according to the theory, only when all the other needs have been met.

The precise implications of this view for learning at school are not entirely clear. On the one hand, it might appear that full attention to school learning tasks will only be possible for those children whose other needs are fully satisfied, in which case they can direct their energies to meeting the need to 'know and understand'. On the other hand, success at school tasks may help a child to achieve other needs, for instance for self-esteem, or even love and belonging. In this case it is harder to specify the circumstances in which a particular child will concentrate on school learning.

Achievement Motivation

The desire to achieve is widespread, but the forms it takes differ not only between people but within the same individual at different times. A number of needs, which vary in strength, combine to form a general *achievement motivation* in learners. David Ausubel (1968) suggests that in school setting achievement motivation has at least three components. The first is *cognitive drive*. This refers to the motivational effects of a learner finding a task interesting, or relating to the individuals need for *competence*. The cognitive drive is 'task-oriented', in that the motive for attending to the task and becoming involved in the activity is intrinsic to the task itself. Some writers have claimed that schooling tends to destroy children's curiosity and the interest in learning that they display when they first enter school (Bruner, 1972; Bates, 1979).

The second component of achievement motivation in the classroom is an *ego-enhancing* one. For Ausubel, ego-enhancing factors are ones that refer to learners' feelings about status, self-esteem, being adequate and having success. These factors can motivate learning, but indirectly, through events that are external to the actual learning task, such as high marks, praise and other rewards. These factors can undoubtedly have a positive influence on learning, albeit an indirect one. However, since they largely depend upon other people, they do not make a contribution to the individual student's independence and self-control as a learner.

Thirdly, there are *affiliative* components of achievement motivation. These are directed towards bringing a person the approval of others. This source of influence may add to or oppose the effect of the other factors that contribute to achievement motivation. For instance, acting in a way that is designed to win the admiration of a child's peers and be accepted as 'one of the gang' may be incompatible with study behaviour activated by the cognitive drive.

Each of the three components of achievement motivation, cognitive, ego-enhancing and affiliative, can vary in both strength and direction. Their relative strengths change as children get older. In young children, for instance, the affiliative drive is very strong, and the attention of adults is important for them. That is one reason for the success of those *behaviour modification* techniques for classroom management in which the teacher's attention is contingent on good behaviour. In older children, the need for the teacher's attention is less strong, and consequently such techniques are considerably less effective. For the older child, the attention and approval of other pupils is likely to be at least as important as the teacher's attention.

Being and Feeling in Control

A child's achievements are influenced by the extent to which he feels in control of his own learning processes. A number of factors, beginning in infancy, affect the young person's feeling of being in control. In the infant, the fact that responses are seen to have predictable outcomes contributes towards the beginnings of a sense of having mastery over the environment, rather than being entirely helpless. One writer has noted in his own infant the synchrony between responses and outcomes that is essential if a child is to start to gain a sense of control:

> He sucks, the world responds with warm milk. He pats the breast, his mother tenderly squeezes him back. He takes a break and coos, his mother coos back. He gives a happy chirp, his mother attempts to chirp back. Each step he takes is synchronized with a response from the world. (Seligman, 1975, p. 139)

Learned helplessness

Normally, the child learns that in a gradually increasing range of circumstances his own actions matter: they have outcomes that influence the environment. But, for a variety of reasons, individual differences arise in children's experiences of control over their own lives. Extreme instances of lack of such control are found in what Martin Seligman (1975) terms *learned helplessness*. Seligman has drawn attention to the results of experiments on human and animal subjects showing that when an organism does *not* have control over what happens to it, and learns that it has no control, it becomes unresponsive and passive, learns poorly and fails to display normal social behaviours.

Some of the symptoms that we associate with the state of depression in adults are regarded by Seligman as being related to learned helplessness. He notes some similarities between the behaviour of a depressed person – isolated, withdrawn, passive and indecisive – and the behaviour of animals in whom learned helplessness has been induced by placing them in circumstances in which their actions are not reliably followed by predictable outcomes, and thus exert no effective control over the environment.

Locus of Control

The above account is a controversial one in some respects, but there is little doubt that the extent to which a child is able to control various aspects of life is important for later development, as is the extent to which he *feels* himself to be in control. A number of researchers have examined the implications for school learning of a child's beliefs about the control of events. The concept of *locus of control* refers to a person's general expectancy for events that affect the individual to be controlled by internal or external factors (Rotter, 1975). A person perceives control to be internal when he believes that events or outcomes depend on his own behaviour or personal characteristics, such as ability. A person is said to perceive events as being externally controlled if he believes them to be caused by factors that are beyond his control, such as luck, fate or the actions of other people.

A child's perceptions about locus of control are largely determined by past experiences. Equally importantly, perceptions about locus of control affect the child's approach to learning. The belief by a child that the outcome of a situation depends on his or her own actions makes it more likely that the child will introduce and persist at those kinds of behaviour that lead to successful learning. Such a child will be more likely to attend to the task, to rehearse, to introduce appropriate learning strategies, and so on, than a child who believes that outcomes and rewards are caused by external factors.

The perceived locus of control is not the only factor influencing a child's approach to a task. The child's perception of the value of the outcome is equally crucial. A child may believe (correctly) that the chances of getting high marks in a test depend upon the time spent studying, but unless the same child places a high value upon a good test score this perception may fail to influence studying (Stipek and Weisz, 1981).

Locus of control is correlated with school achievement: high achievement levels are associated with the perception of control as being internal. However, although this finding is consistent with the view that perceiving control to be internal positively influences achievement at school, it is not inevitable that any such cause-and-effect relationship exists. Conceivably, the correlation could be due to achievements having an influence on perceived locus of control, or to both factors being affected by some (unknown) third variable. It is possible, for instance, that when children are successful at school they perceive themselves as being the cause of their success (internal control) whereas when they are less successful they blame outside influences (external locus of control).

As it happens, the findings of carefully controlled studies that have been undertaken to examine this and other possibilities show that locus of control does influence achievement. This does not entirely rule out the additional possibility that achievement may have some effect upon perceived locus of control, but the main influence is in the opposite direction.

The effects of altered locus of control

If a child's perceptions of locus of control can be altered, it ought to be possible to raise school achievement. Does this actually happen? Some interesting classroom experiments have shown that changing children's perceptions of control can have exciting positive effects. In one study (Matheny and Edwards, 1974) 25 classroom teachers followed careful instructions to give the young children greater responsibility for organizing their own learning activities. This led to a very large improvement in performance at reading, and it was also noted that the largest effects occurred in classrooms where the teachers were judged to have been most successful in following the instructions.

In another classroom experiment six-year-old children who had previously been told by the teacher exactly when to do various kinds of school work were allowed to decide for themselves on the timing of the various tasks, although the choice of the tasks remained with the teacher (Wang and Stiles, 1976). The change resulted in a higher proportion of assignments being completed. Allowing children to choose for themselves the order in which tasks were done also gave them an increased feeling of control (as indicated by interview reports) over their learning at school.

Findings such as these demonstrate that giving children greater control over their educational experiences can lead to very real improvements in school learning. There are some uncertainties concerning the detailed interpretation of the results. For example, it is not entirely clear whether the beneficial effects are due to differences in locus of control as such, or to differences in *perception* of control locus, or to both, or to other factors that the experiments failed to control. Whatever the answers, however, it is very likely that the factors manipulated in studies of classroom control are ones that are of great practical importance.

Another incompletely resolved issue concerns the possibility that different types of internal and external control have different effects. For example, Stipek and Weisz (1981) note that an analysis based on attribution theory would point to the fact that a child who thinks that his failure is due to lack of ability (perceived internal locus of control) will act differently after failure at a learning task than a child who thinks that the failure is due to not trying (again, perceived internal locus of control).

Student mastery and locus of control. It is highly probable that the effectiveness of a variety of successful educational experiments, innovations and reforms has been due at least in part to children gaining greater control over the circumstances in which they learn. Instances include the beneficial effects associated with mastery learning and (observed in some investigations, but not all) with open-plan classrooms. An especially important element of changes in the locus of control is the fact that individuals are allowed to make choices for themselves. Altered perceptions of control may have been a key factor in the success of a project in which high-school student volunteers, who were themselves poor readers, were paid to tutor younger backward readers (Cloward, 1967). The most striking finding was not that the younger children's reading scores improved (they actually gained six months' growth over a five-month period in which they were tutored four hours per week, compared with 3.5 months' growth, on average, by students in a control group), but that the tutors' own reading standard improved considerably. The tutors' gained an average of 3.4 years in reading skills, over the seven-month period during which they participated in the experiment, compared with a gain of 1.7 years by students in a control condition. Almost certainly, gains in self-esteem and the shift that the experiment brought about towards greater student control over reading activities contributed to this very real improvement.

Pawns and origins. Another classroom investigation of the effects of changing children's perceptions of locus of control was undertaken by R. de Charms (1976), who makes the distinction between perceiving oneself as a 'pawn' who is controlled largely by external forces or as an 'origin'. An origin is a person who regards his actions as being caused by his own free choices and wishes, and consequently assumes responsibility for his activities and achievements.

De Charms considers that schooling influences children's perceptions of themselves as being pawns or origins. To test some of his ideas he conducted an experiment in which black inner-city children (aged 12 to 14 years) in the United States were encouraged to assume more control of their own activities in the classroom and to take responsibility for their own actions. Their teachers were trained to teach the children to perceive themselves as being origins, and largely in charge of their own lives and responsible for their successes and failures, rather than being pawns, and mere instruments of outside influences. The teaching was not only effective in altering the children's thinking about themselves in the direction of greater emphasis on their being origins rather than pawns, but it also had a positive influence on school achievement.

Success and Failure in the Classroom

Closely related to a person's perceptions about the factors that control important aspects of life are experiences of success and failure. It was mentioned previously that one beneficial effect of mastery learning is to induce an increased feeling of being personally in control over learning experiences. At least equally important are the effects on a person's self-perceptions of failing or being successful. Experiences of succeeding or failing inevitably contribute to a child's assessments of his own ability and to expectancies concerning success in the future. The very perceptions that we have regarded as forming barriers to a child's being successful at school, that is, of being externally controlled or of having the role of a pawn rather than an origin, can alternatively be seen as providing effective devices for maintaining one's self-esteem. If one is constantly failing, it is comforting to believe that forces outside one's control are responsible.

Investigating the effects of classroom failure

What happens to a child at school who encounters failure after failure? Some indications are given by the results of an experiment in which the subjects experienced repeated failure (Covington and Omelich, 1981). In fact, failure led to the participants having lower estimates of their ability, and in turn they became less happy, more shameful and less confident of future success. With the accumulation of further failures they became increasingly distressed, they experienced feelings of hopelessness and they became anxious to attribute their failure to external factors if it was at all possible to do so. When other strategies for maintaining self-esteem in the face of failure were no longer effective, signs of inaction and hopelessness became common.

The investigators note that a strategy of being inactive, which is not uncommonly observed in children at school by frustrated teachers and which might seem to be self-defeating, since it usually leads to failure, is actually very effective for some children. Such a strategy 'at least offsets the personal, shame-evoking implications of low ability' (Covington and Omelich, 1981, p. 806). For a student who has little confidence in success, is anxious not to fail in future attempts to learn, and is perhaps not particularly interested in the topic being studied, being passive may well be the best way of dealing with the situation.

It is worth drawing attention to the fact that the participants in the above experiment were college students: the effects of failure on young children or individuals who are less knowledgeable and less confident about their learning abilities might well have been even more devastating. It is also pertinent that although the duration of the experiment was relatively long – several weeks – the time span was considerably less than that in which failures can mount in a child's day-to-day experience of life at school.

References

Atkinson, R. C. 1975. Mnemotechnics in second-language learning. *American Psychologist* 30: 821–8.

Ausubel D. P. 1968. *Educational Psychology: A Cognitive View*. New York: Holt, Rinehart & Winston.

Bartlett, F. C. 1932. *Remembering*. Cambridge, England: Cambridge University Press.

Bates, J. A. 1979. Extrinsic reward and intrinsic motivation: a review with implications for the classroom. *Review of Educational Research* 49: 557–76.

Belmont, J. M. 1978. Individual differences in memory: the cases of normal and retarded development. In M. M. Gruneberg and P. E. Morris (eds), *Aspects of Memory*. London: Methuen.

Benjamin, H. 1939. *The Sabre-Tooth Curriculum*. New York: McGraw-Hill.

Bennett, H. L. 1983. Remembering drink orders: the memory skills of cocktail waitresses. *Human Learning: Journal of Practical Research and Applications* 2: 157–70.

Bereiter, C., and Scardamalia, M. 1982. From conversation to composition: the role of instruction in a developmental process. In R. Glaser (ed.), *Advances in Instructional Psychology*, vol. 2. Hillsdale, New Jersey: Erlbaum.

Biggs, J. B., and Telfer, R. 1981. *The Process of Learning*. Sydney: Prentice-Hall.

Block, J. H. 1971. *Mastery Learning: Theory and Practice*. New York: Holt, Rinehart & Winston.

Bloom, B. S. (ed.) 1956. *Taxonomy of Educational Objectives. Handbook One: Cognitive Domain*. New York: David McKay.

Bloom, B. S. 1974. Time and learning. *American Psychologist* 29: 682–8.

Bloom, B. S. 1976. *Human Characteristics and School Learning*. New York: McGraw-Hill.

Bower, G. H., and Clark, M. C. 1969. Narrative stories as mediators of serial learning. *Psychonomic Science* 14: 181–2.

Bower, G. H., and Karlin, M. B. 1974. Depth of processing pictures of faces and recognition memory. *Journal of Experimental Psychology* 103: 751–7.

Brainerd C. J. 1977. Cognitive development and concept learning: an interpretative review. *Psychological Bulletin* 84: 919–39.

Bransford, J. D., Nitsch, K. E., and Franks, J. J. 1977. Schooling and the facilitation of knowing. In R. C. Anderson, R. J. Spiro, and W. E. Montague (eds), *Schooling and the Acquisition of Knowledge*. Hillsdale, New Jersey: Erlbaum.

Bransford, J. D., Stein, B. S., Shelton, T. S., and Owings, R. A. 1981. Cognition and adaptation: the importance of learning to learn. In J. H. Harvey (ed.), *Cognition, Social Behavior, and the Environment*. Hillsdale, New Jersey: Erlbaum.

Brewer, W. F., and Dupree, D. A. 1983. Use of plan schemata in the recall and recognition of goal-directed actions. *Journal of Experimental Psychology: Learning, Memory, and Cognition* 9: 117–29.

Brown, A. L., and Day, J. D. 1983. Macrorules for summarizing texts: the development of expertise. *Journal of Verbal Learning and Verbal Behavior* 22: 1–14.

Brown, A. L., Palincsar, A. S., and Armbruster, B. B. 1984. Instructing comprehension-fostering activities in interactive learning situations. In H. Mandl, N. Stein and T. Trabasso (eds), *Learning and Comprehension of Texts*. Hillsdale, New Jersey: Erlbaum.

Brown, A. L. and Smiley, S. S. 1978. The development of strategies for studying texts. *Child Development* 49: 1076–1088.

Bruner, J. S. 1972. Nature and uses of immaturity. *American Psychologist* 27: 687–707,

Butterfield, E. C., Wambold, C., and Belmont, J. M. 1973. On theory and practice of improving short-term memory. *American Journal of Mental Deficiency* 77: 654–69.

Ceci, S. J., Caves, R. T., and Howe, M. J. A. 1981. Children's long-term memory for information that is incongruous with their prior knowledge. *British Journal of Psychology* 72: 443–50.

Ceci, S. J., and Howe, M. J. A. 1978. Semantic knowledge as a determinant of developmental differences in recall. *Journal of Experimental Child Psychology* 26: 230–45.

Chase, W. G., and Ericsson, K. A. 1981. Skilled memory. In J. Anderson (ed.), *Cognitive Skills and their Acquisition*. Hillsdale, New Jersey: Erlbaum.

Chi, M. T. H. 1978. Knowledge structures and memory development. In R. Siegler (ed.), *Children's Thinking: What Develops?* Hillsdale, New Jersey: Erlbaum.

Chi, M. T. H., and Koeske, R. D. 1983. Network representation of a child's dinosaur knowledge. *Developmental Psychology* 19: 29–39.

Clarke, A. M., and Clarke, A. D. B. 1976. *Early Experience: Myth and Evidence*. London: Open Books.

Cloward, R. D. 1967. Studies in tutoring. *Journal of Experimental Education* 36: 14–25.

Cole, M., Gay, J., Glick, J. A., and Sharp, D. W. 1971. *The Cultural Context of Learning and Thinking.* New York: Basic Books.

Collins, A., and Quillian, M. R. 1969. Retrieval time from semantic memory. *Journal of Verbal Learning and Verbal Behavior* 8: 240–47.

Collins, A., and Quillian, M. R. 1972. How to make a language user. In E. Tulving and W. Donaldson (eds), *Organization of Memory.* New York: Academic Press.

Collins, A., and Smith, E. E. 1982. Teaching the process of reading comprehension. In D. K. Detterman and R. J. Sternberg (eds), *How and How Much Can Intelligence Be Increased?* Norwood, New Jersey: Ablex.

Conrad, C. 1972. Cognitive economy in semantic memory. *Journal of Experimental Psychology* 92: 149–54.

Covington, M. L., and Omelich, C. L. 1981. As failures mount: affective and cognitive consequences of ability demotion in the classroom. *Journal of Educational Psychology* 73: 796–808.

Craik, F. I. M., and Lockhart, R. S. 1972. Levels of processing: a framework for memory research. *Journal of Verbal Learning and Verbal Behavior* 12: 599–607.

Craik, F. I. M., and Tulving, E. 1975. Depth of processing and the retention of words in episodic memory. *Journal of Experimental Psychology: General* 104: 268–94.

de Charms, R. 1976. *Enhancing Motivation: Change in the Classroom.* New York: Halsted.

Donaldson, M. 1978. *Children's Minds.* London: Fontana.

Dooling, D. J., and Lachman, R. 1971. Effects of comprehension on retention of prose. *Journal of Experimental Psychology* 88: 216–22.

Duchastel, P. C. 1982. Testing effects measured with alternate test forms. *Educational Research* 75: 309–13.

Entwistle, N. J., and Cunningham, S. 1968. Neuroticism and school achievement: a linear relationship? *British Journal of Educational Psychology* 38: 123–32.

Escalona, S. K. 1973. The differential impact of environmental conditions as a function of different reaction patterns in infancy. In J. C. Westman (ed.), *Individual Differences in Children.* New York: Wiley.

Estes, W. K. 1970. *Learning Theory and Mental Development.* New York: Academic Press.

Feuerstein, R. 1979. *The Dynamic Assessment of Retarded Performers: The Learning Potential Assessment Device, Theory, Instruments, and Techniques.* Baltimore, Maryland: University Park Press.

Flavell, J. H., Beach, D. R., and Chinsky, J. M. 1966. Spontaneous verbal rehearsal in a memory task as a function of age. *Child Development* 37: 324–40.

Fontana, D. 1981. *Psychology for Teachers.* London: The British Psychological Society/Macmillan.

Gagne, R. M. 1968. Contributions of learning to human development. *Journal of Educational Psychology* 60: 408–14.

Gagne, R. M. 1970. *The Conditions of Learning* (2nd edn). New York: Holt, Rinehart & Winston.

Gagne, R. M., and Dick, W. 1983. Instructional psychology. *Annual Review of Psychology* 43: 261–95.

Gates, A. I. 1917. Recitation as a factor in memorizing. *Archives of Psychology* 6: Number 40.

Glaser, R. 1982. Instructional psychology: past, present and future. *American Psychologist* 37: 292–305.

Gruneberg, M. M. 1973. The role of memorization techniques in finals examination preparation: a study of psychology students. *Educational Research* 16: 134–39.

Hartley, J., and Cameron, A. 1967. Some observations on the efficiency of lecturing. *Education Review* 20: 30–7

Higbee, K. L., and Millard, R. J. 1981. Effects of imagery value and an imagery mnemonic on memory for sayings. *Bulletin of the Psychonomic Society* 17: 215–16.

Howe, M. J. A. 1970. Repeated presentation and recall of meaningful prose. *Journal of Educational Psychology* 61: 214–19.

Howe, M. J. A. 1975. *Learning in Infants and Young Children*. London: Macmillan.

Howe, M. J. A. 1977. Learning and the acquisition of knowledge by students: some experimental investigations. In M. J. A. Howe (ed.), *Adult Learning: Psychological Research and Applications*. London: Wiley.

Howe, M. J. A. 1980. *The Psychology of Human Learning*. New York: Harper & Row.

Howe, M. J. A., and Godfrey, J. 1977. *Student Note-taking as an Aid to Learning*. Exeter, England: Exeter University Teaching Services.

Hyde, T. S., and Jenkins, J. J. 1969. Differential effects of incidental tasks on the organization of recall of a list of highly associated words. *Journal of Experimental Psychology* 82: 472–81.

Jensen, A. R. 1978. The nature of intelligence and its relation to learning. In S. Murray-Smith (ed.), *Melbourne Studies in Education*. Victoria, Australia: Melbourne University Press.

Kasper, L. F. 1983. The effect of linking sentence and interactive picture mnemonics on the acquisition of Spanish nouns by middle school children. *Human Learning: Journal of Practical Research and Applications* 2: 141–56.

Kintsch, W. 1975. Memory for prose. In C. N. Cofer (ed.), *The Structure of Human Memory*. San Francisco: Freeman.

Kobigasigawa, A. 1974. Utilization of retrieval cues by children in recall. *Child Development* 45: 40–6.

Korner, A. F. 1971. Individual differences at birth: implications for early experience and later development. *American Journal of Orthopsychiatry* 41: 608–19.

Lakoff, G., and Johnson, M. 1980. *Metaphors We Live By*. Chicago: University of Chicago Press.

Levin, J. R., McCormick, C. B., Miller, G. E., Berry, J. K., and Pressley, M. 1982. Mnemonic versus non-mnemonic vocabulary learning strategies for children. *American Educational Research Journal* 19: 121–36.

Loehlin, J. C., Vandenberg, S. G., and Osborne, R. T. 1973. Blood group genes and negro-white ability differences. *Behavior Genetics* 26: 400–11.

Loftus, E. F., and Palmer, J. C. 1974. Reconstruction of automobile destruction: an example of the interaction between language and memory. *Journal of Verbal Learning and Verbal Behavior* 13: 585–89.

Loftus, G. R., and and Loftus, E. F. 1983. *Mind at Play: The Psychology of Video Games*. New York: Basic Books.

McGuire, T. R., and Hirsch, J. 1977. General intelligence and heritability. In I. C. Uzgiris and F. Weizmann (eds), *The Structuring of Experience*. New York: Plenum Press.

Marjoribanks, K. 1977. Socioeconomic status and its relation to cognitive performance as mediated through the family environment. In A. Oliveiro (ed.), *Genetics, environment and intelligence*. Amsterdam: Elsevier/North Holland Biomedical Press.

Markman, E. 1979. Realizing that you don't understand: elementary school children's awareness of inconsistencies. *Child Development* 50: 643–55.

Marton, F. 1981. Phenomenography – describing conceptions of the world around us. *Instructional Science* 10: 177–200.

Matheny, K., and Edwards, C. 1974. Academic improvement through an experimental classroom management system. *Journal of School Psychology* 12: 222–32.

Miller, G. A. 1956. The magical number seven, plus or minus two: some limits on our capacity for processing information. *Psychological Review* 63: 81–97.

Pressley, G. M. 1977. Children's use of the keyword method to learn simple Spanish vocabulary words. *Journal of Educational Psychology* 69: 465–72.

Raugh, M. R., and Atkinson, R. C. 1975. A mnemonic method for learning a second language vocabulary. *Journal of Educational Psychology* 67: 1–16.

Rips, L. J., Shoben, E. J., and Smith, E. E. 1973. Semantic distance and the verification of semantic relations. *Journal of Verbal Learning and Verbal Behaviour* 12: 1–20.

Rogers, T. B., Kuiper, N. A., and Kirker, W. S. 1977. Self-references and the encoding of personal information. *Journal of Personality and Social Psychology* 35: 677–88.

Rothkopf, E. Z. 1970. The concept of mathemagenic activities. *Review of Educational Research* 40: 325–36.

Rotter, J. 1975. Some problems and misconceptions related to the construct of internal versus external control of reinforcement. *Journal of Consulting and Clinical Psychology* 43: 56–67.

Rozin, P. 1976. The evolution of intelligence and access to the cognitive unconscious. *Progress in Psychobiology, Physiology and Psychology* 6: 245–80.

Scardamalia, M. 1981. How children cope with the cognitive demands of writing. In C. H. Frederikson and J. F. Dominic (eds), *Writing: The Nature, Development and Teaching of Written Communication. Vol. 2: Writing: Process, Development and Communication*. Hillsdale, New Jersey: Erlbaum.

Schaffer, H. R., and Emerson, P. E. 1964. Patterns of response to physical contact in early human development. *Journal of Child Psychology and Psychiatry* 5: 1–13.

Schank, R. C., and Abelson, R. P. 1977. *Scripts, Plans, Goals and Understanding: An Inquiry Into Human Knowledge Structures*. Hillsdale, New Jersey: Erlbaum.

Seligman, M. E. P. 1975. *Helplessness: On Depression, Development and Death*. San Francisco: Freeman.

Skinner, B. F. 1938. *The Behavior of Organisms: an Experimental Analysis*. New York: Prentice-Hall.

Snyder, M., and Uranowitz, S. W. 1978. Reconstructing the past: some cognitive consequences of person perception. *Journal of Personality and Social Psychology* 36: 940–60.

Stevenson, H. W., Parker, T., and Wilkinson, A. 1975. Ratings and measures of memory processes in young children. Unpublished manuscript. University of Michigan.

Stipek, D. J., and Weisz, J. R. 1981. Perceived personal control and academic achievement. *Review of Educational Research* 51: 101–37.

Sweeney, C. A., and Bellezza, F. S. 1982. Use of the keyword mnemonic in learning English vocabulary. *Human Learning: Journal of Practical Research and Applications* 1: 155–64.

Thompson, R. F. 1976. The search for the engram. *American Psychologist* 31: 209–27.

Thorndike, E. L. 1931. *Human learning*. New York: Prentice-Hall.

Turnure, J., Buium, N., and Thurlow, M. 1976. The effectiveness of interrogatives for promoting verbal elaboration productivity in young children. *Child Development* 11: 780–7.

Wachs, T. D., and Gruen, G. E. 1982. *Early Experience and Human Development*. New York: Plenum Press.

Wang, M., and Stiles, B. 1976. An investigation of children's concept of self-responsibility for their school learning. *American Educational Research Journal* 13: 159–79.

Wells, C. G. 1981. Some antecedents of early educational attainment. *British Journal of Sociology of Education* 2: 181–200.

White, B. L. 1971. *Human Infants: Experience and Psychological Development.* Englewood Cliffs, New Jersey: Prentice Hall.

White, R. T. 1979. Achievement, mastery, proficiency, competence. *Studies in Science Education* 6: 1–22.

Zajonc, R. 1976. Family configuration and intelligence. *Science* 192: 227–36.

Index